**T&T CLARK STUDY GUIDES TO THE OLD TESTAMENT**

# Leviticus: The Priestly Vision of Holiness

Series Editor

Adrian Curtis, University of Manchester, UK

Published in association with the Society for Old Testament Study

Other titles in the series include:

Amos: An Introduction and Study Guide

1 & 2 Kings: An Introduction and Study Guide

1 & 2 Samuel: An Introduction and Study Guide

Ecclesiastes: An Introduction and Study Guide

Exodus: An Introduction and Study Guide

Ezra-Nehemiah: An Introduction and Study Guide

Hebrews: An Introduction and Study Guide

Lamentations: An Introduction and Study Guide

Leviticus: An Introduction and Study Guide

Jeremiah: An Introduction and Study Guide

Job: An Introduction and Study Guide

Joel, Obadiah, Habakkuk, Zephaniah: An Introduction and Study Guide

Joshua: An Introduction and Study Guide

Psalms: An Introduction and Study Guide

Song of Songs: An Introduction and Study Guide

Numbers: An Introduction and Study Guide

## T&T CLARK STUDY GUIDES TO THE NEW TESTAMENT

1 & 2 Thessalonians: An Introduction and Study Guide

1 Peter: An Introduction and Study Guide

2 Corinthians: An Introduction and Study Guide

Colossians: An Introduction and Study Guide

Ephesians: An Introduction and Study Guide

Galatians: An Introduction and Study Guide

James: An Introduction and Study Guide

John: An Introduction and Study Guide

Luke: An Introduction and Study Guide

Mark: An Introduction and Study Guide

Matthew: An Introduction and Study Guide

Philemon: An Introduction and Study Guide

# Leviticus: The Priestly Vision of Holiness

## An Introduction and Study Guide

**Philip Peter Jenson**

t&tclark

LONDON • NEW YORK • OXFORD • NEW DELHI • SYDNEY

T&T CLARK
Bloomsbury Publishing Plc
50 Bedford Square, London, WC1B 3DP, UK
1385 Broadway, New York, NY 10018, USA
29 Earlsfort Terrace, Dublin 2, Ireland

BLOOMSBURY, T&T CLARK and the T&T Clark logo are trademarks of
Bloomsbury Publishing Plc

First published in Great Britain 2021

Cover design by clareturner.co.uk

A catalogue record for this book is available from the British Library.

Library of Congress Cataloging-in-Publication Data
Names: Jenson, Philip Peter, author.
Title: Leviticus : an introduction and study guide / by Philip Peter Jenson.
Description: London ; New York : T&T Clark, 2021. | Series: T&T Clark's study guides to
the Old Testament | Includes bibliographical references and index. | Summary: "Philip
Peter Jenson provides an introduction to the Book of Leviticus in the Old Testament,
examining the book's structure and characteristics; covering the latest biblical
scholarship, including historical and interpretive issues; and considering a range of
scholarly approaches. Each chapter concludes with brief reflections on the
contemporary significance of the texts being discussed. In particular, this guide focuses
on explaining the underlying concepts that inform the laws and rituals of Leviticus. With
suggestions of further reading at the end of each chapter, this guide will be an useful
accompaniment to study of the Book of Leviticus"– Provided by publisher.
Identifiers: LCCN 2021001257 (print) | LCCN 2021001258 (ebook) | ISBN
9780567693617 (hardback) | ISBN 9780567674838 (paperback) | ISBN
9780567674845 (pdf) | ISBN 9780567674852 (epub)
Subjects: LCSH: Bible. Leviticus–Introductions. | Bible. Leviticus–Study
and teaching.
Classification: LCC BS1255.55 .J46 2021 (print) | LCC BS1255.55 (ebook) |
DDC 222/.13061–dc23
LC record available at https://lccn.loc.gov/2021001257
LC ebook record available at https://lccn.loc.gov/2021001258

ISBN:    HB:     978-0-5676-9361-7
         PB:     978-0-5676-7483-8
         ePDF:   978-0-5676-7484-5
         eBook:  978-0-5676-7485-2

Series: T&T Clark Study Guides to the Old Testament

Typeset by Integra Software Services Pvt. Ltd.

To find out more about our authors and books visit www.bloomsbury.com
and sign up for our newsletters

# Contents

# Figures

# Abbreviations

| | |
|---|---|
| ABD | Anchor Bible Dictionary |
| ANE | Ancient Near East |
| *Bib* | *Biblica* |
| BZAW | Beihefte zur *Zeitschrift für die Alttestamentliche Wissenschaft* |
| FAT | Forschungen zum Alten Testament |
| Heb. | Hebrew (verse numbers in Masoretic Text) |
| HThKAT | Herders Theologischer Kommentar zum Alten Testament |
| *JAOS* | *Journal of the American Oriental Society* |
| *JBL* | *Journal of Biblical Literature* |
| JPS | Jewish Publication Society |
| *JSOT* | *Journal for the Study of the Old Testament* |
| JSOTSup | *Journal for the Study of the Old Testament* Supplement Series |
| LHBOTS | Library of Hebrew Bible/Old Testament Studies |
| NJPS | New Jewish Publication Society |
| NRSV | *New Revised Standard Version* |
| OTL | Old Testament Library |
| *RB* | *Revue Biblique* |
| SBLDS | Society of Biblical Literature Dissertation Series |
| *VT* | *Vetus Testamentum* |
| VTSup | *Vetus Testamentum*, Supplements |
| *ZAW* | *Zeitschrift für die alttestamentliche Wissenschaft* |

# Series Preface

How can a potential reader be sure that a Guide to a biblical book is balanced and reliable? One answer is 'If the Guide has been produced under the auspices of an organisation such as the Society for Old Testament Study.'

Founded in 1917, the Society for Old Testament Study (or SOTS as it is commonly known) is a British and Irish society for Old Testament scholars, but with a world-wide membership. It seeks to foster the academic study of the Old Testament/Hebrew Bible in various ways, for example by arranging Conferences (usually twice per year) for its members, maintaining links with other learned societies with similar interests in the British Isles and abroad, and producing a range of publications, including scholarly monographs, and collections of essays by individual authors or on specific topics. Periodically it has published volumes seeking to provide an overview of recent developments and emphases in the discipline at the time of publication. The annual Society for Old Testament Study Book List, containing succinct reviews by members of the Society of works on the Old Testament and related areas which have been published in the previous year or so, has proved an invaluable bibliographical resource.

With the needs of students in particular in mind, the Society also produced a series of Study Guides to the books of the Old Testament. This first series of Old Testament Guides, published for the Society by Sheffield Academic Press in the 1980s and 1990s, under the general editorship of the late Professor Norman Whybray, was well received as a very useful resource which teachers could recommend to their students with confidence. But it has inevitably become dated with the passage of time, hence the decision that a new series should be commissioned.

The aim of the new series is to continue the tradition established by the first Series, namely to provide a concise, comprehensive, manageable and affordable guide to each biblical book. The intention is that each volume will contain an authoritative overview of the current thinking on the traditional matters of Old Testament/Hebrew Bible introduction, addressing matters of content, major critical issues, and theological perspectives, in the light of recent scholarship, and suggesting suitable further reading. Where appropriate to the particular biblical book or books, attention may also be given to less traditional approaches or particular theoretical perspectives.

All the authors are members of the Society, known for their scholarship and with wide experience of teaching in Universities and Colleges. The series general editor, Adrian Curtis, taught Old Testament/Hebrew Bible at the University of Manchester for many years, is a former Secretary of the Society, and was President of the Society for 2016.

It is the hope of the Society that these Guides will stimulate in their readers an appreciation of the body of literature whose study is at the heart of all its activities.

# 1

# Reading Leviticus

## The challenge of Leviticus

Anyone approaching Leviticus for the first time is likely to find it a difficult book to read and understand. Those used to reading flowing narrative will be frustrated by its repetitive style and content. The customs and practices it details largely belong to an ancient past. Most readers in the West have never seen an animal sacrifice, and the concept of physical impurity is alien to modernity. Yet this is also the book that is at the heart of the Pentateuch, the foundation of the Jewish and Christian scriptures. The issues that Leviticus addresses are of perennial concern: how an imperfect and sinful people can worship a holy God, how the people of God should relate to insiders and outsiders, and how they are to know God's blessing in the place where they live. Even though the world of Leviticus no longer exists, the principles and goals underlying its laws and regulations may provide illumination and insight. This is especially the case if the final editing of Leviticus took place in a world in which its setting and rituals were as theoretical as they are today. Those responsible considered it an abiding and instructive word for the people of God.

The scholarly study of Leviticus has sought to make sense of it by applying the full range of interpretive methods that are employed in biblical studies (Barton 1984; Tate 2008). For the last 200 years the dominant interest has been to explain its complex character from a historical point of view. For example, what were the sources of the different parts of Leviticus, when are they to be dated, and how did the book become what we have today? These questions about the *world behind the text* are inseparable from the larger debate about the sources and the formation of the Pentateuch.

More recently interest has turned to taking seriously the *world of the text* as well-crafted literature, whatever its historical origins. Can we discern an overarching structure for the book? Is there an underlying rationale for the myriad instructions relating to impurity? Is there consistency between the perspective of Leviticus 1–16 and 17–27? Literary explanations can be in tension with the historical approach. If different texts indicate different points of view (e.g. on the nature of holiness), is this because they derive from different sources, or because they are partial expressions of a more comprehensive system, or can both explanations be valid?

However, throughout history most readers of Leviticus have been believers, regarding the book as canonical holy scripture. However difficult the text appears to be, it is there because it reveals important aspects of God's character and his will. Leviticus was not written for historians or literary critics, but to shape the lives of obedient readers through its communicative artistry and theological truth. The *world in front of the text* also includes all subsequent readers, especially the contemporary community of faith. Reader-oriented approaches explore the complex two-way interaction between the world of the text and the world of the reader. Such readers will indeed have many questions about it (the hermeneutic of suspicion), but this is the beginning of a critical journey that they wager will eventually lead to deepened understanding and a return to the fullness of the text (the hermeneutic of trust; Ricœur 1967:347–57). Others, though, may wish to question or dispute the fundamental assumptions and claims of the text about God's will for his people. It is possible to read the text 'against the grain' and propose a different way to understanding reality.

The major commentaries and studies on Leviticus generally focus on one or other of these worlds, though not without reference to the others. Historical critical study is the primary concern of Noth (1965), Elliger (1966), Budd (1996) and Nihan (2007). More recent commentaries (Rendtorff 2004; Willis 2009; Watts 2013) direct most of their energies to expounding the final form of the text. More explicit discussion of how the text relates contemporary faith and practice is found in Christian (Wenham 1979; Hartley 1992; Balentine 2002; Gane 2004; Radner 2008; Hieke 2014) and Jewish commentaries (Levine 1989; Milgrom 1990; 2000; 2001).

# The sources of Leviticus

We probe these worlds of the text in a little more detail. In recent historical scholarship, Leviticus represented a prime witness for the Priestly writing (P), a reasonably neutral designation for what has otherwise been called the Priestly source, author, tradition, or circle. In this guide a capital letter (Priestly) will distinguish reference to this tradition from that which concerns priests (priestly). Analysing the Pentateuch as a combination of sources began in the nineteenth century, when scholars began to question the traditional authorship of Moses. They pointed to numerous inconsistencies of language, style and content that were hard to attribute to one figure. In the documentary hypothesis, which has until recently been the dominant model, the Pentateuch consisted of four main independent sources that were eventually joined together by redactors. J (from the German *Jahvist*) was so called because it was understood as assuming that the special name of God was known from the beginning (Gen. 4:26). This name is normally rendered in English translations as the Lord, but Yhwh, a transliteration of its four Hebrew consonants, will be used in this guide. The Elohist (E), on the other hand, referred to the general title God (Elohim) in Genesis until the divine name was revealed at the Exodus (Exod. 3:13-14). The same view was attributed to the P source, which is responsible for a second account of the revelation of the name (Exod. 6:3). D, mainly represented by Deuteronomy, was marked by a distinctive rhetorical style. The order of the sources that was eventually agreed upon was J → E → D → P. The story of the rise of this hypothesis, its variants and its recent questioning lies beyond the scope of this introduction (Carr 2011; Dozeman 2017). Very few experts in the field now regard the classical exposition as accurate, although the hold of the previous consensus remains strong.

The source critics, especially in the German tradition, were not satisfied with a simple P. The documentary hypothesis had been developed on the basis of the narrative texts in Genesis and Exodus, and those identified as Priestly were called Pg ('g' standing for the German *Grundschrift*, 'basic writing'). The term came about because the first source critics identified it as the earliest source, although Wellhausen persuasively argued that it was instead the latest. However, much of Exodus, Leviticus and Numbers are not narrative, and a large number of priestly rituals and laws were assigned to later Priestly additions. These were referred to as Ps ('s' standing for German *sekundär*, secondary). Later, Priestly redactors continued to add these to the Sinai revelation in order to legitimatize them and emphasize their divine authority. There is a lively discussion about where Pg ends. Some suggested Exodus (Exod. 40), others Leviticus (Lev. 9; 16), Numbers (Num. 36:13), Deuteronomy (Deut. 34:7-9) or even Joshua (Josh. 19:51). However, others began to question whether there should be any sharp division between narrative and law. There is no reason why a tradition cannot incorporate more than one genre. The case can also be made that there is more holding the various Priestly redactions together than that which distinguishes them.

As is typical of historical-critical investigation, P was subject to further analysis, leading to theories of multiple sources and redactions. The number and character of these layers depended on the scholar's sensitivity to differences in vocabulary, form and theology. Elliger's (1966) translation in his commentary is set in an impressive number of fonts, which indicated his view of the complex growth of the text. Milgrom (1991; 2000; 2001) also frequently distinguishes several stages of writing, redaction and interpolation. While it is relatively easy to detect tensions in a chapter, it is far more difficult to determine the origins and dates of underlying sources. Minor differences might be due to a different context, the use of synonyms, or memory variants (Carr 2011). The uncertainty is even greater if a scholar attempts to relate the differences in various chapters to each other and then reconstruct a systematic history of the book's growth. One purpose of attributing all the laws to Moses was to provide a unified and integrated set of laws, so separating layers is a speculative business that goes against the grain of the text. It could be compared with the task of reconstituting the original ingredients of a cake once it has been baked. The lack of consensus regarding the growth of P reflects the difficulty of the enterprise.

# The dating of Leviticus

The classical documentary hypothesis regards P as the latest of the four sources (JEDP). This is a relative dating, but the classic documentary hypothesis associated it with an absolute dating during or shortly after the exile in the sixth century BCE. Some recent scholars have pushed the dating of the final composition even further into the Persian period (Kazen 2015). The most persuasive argument for an exilic or post-exilic dating is the striking absence of evidence for the complex priestly ritual system in pre-exilic texts. This includes some of the specific sacrifices (e.g. the purification offering), the anointing of High Priest, and the distinction between the Aaronic priestly line and those of the other Levitical clans. The editors wished to finalize P so that it could be a blueprint for the restoration of worship when the exiles returned home. The great majority of critical scholars date the final form of Leviticus to the late sixth century or the fifth century BCE.

A minority opinion, especially among Jewish scholars, is that P is pre-exilic. The strongest arguments for this are probably linguistic (Joosten

2016). Various terms and syntactic features in P are said to reflect pre-exilic Classical Biblical Hebrew (CBH) rather than post-exilic Late Biblical Hebrew (LBH) found in texts such as Chronicles (Hurvitz 1988; Milgrom 1991:3–13). For example, Leviticus calls the national assembly an *'ēḏâ* (e.g. Lev. 24:16), whereas Deuteronomy and Ezekiel use exclusively *qāhāl*. Critics point to the difficulties in developing a sound linguistic methodology, and the possible presence of archaizing features, and the presence in P of both earlier and later strata (Blenkinsopp 1996). The discussion is bound up with determining the relative dating of P and H in relation to texts such as Deuteronomy and Ezekiel (Hurvitz 1982; 2000; Lyons 2009).

Wellhausen (1885) proposed a sequential history of religion in which P is the latest source, subsequent and dependent on the earlier sources, and reflecting a post-exilic context and distinct theology. However, the rigidity of the schema has been challenged by various scholars. Weinfeld (1972) argued that P and D reflected different circles or schools rather than different dates. P arose in priestly circles interested in the sanctuary and the worship of Israel; D is the product of scribal circles and treats the worship of Israel in general. Douglas (1999) also proposed a complementary approach: P and D represent two different kinds of thinking, one analogical and comprehensive, the other rational and restricted. They grew and developed alongside each other. Haran (1981) proposed that P reflects a partisan ideal of worship, composed around the time of Ahaz and Hezekiah, which was kept secret and only authorized after the exile.

These different views need not be as far apart as they first appear. Proponents of a pre-exilic date often acknowledge later redactions, while those dating P to post-exilic times readily admit the presence of earlier sources. The extensive perspective represented by P could not have been born overnight, but it is very difficult to tell how extensive its roots are and how far back they might go. A helpful analogy may be the frequent reuse of stones and even walls from older buildings in the construction of new ones. In some areas there may be significant continuity; in others entirely new sections have been added.

# The Holiness Code

The section Leviticus 17–27 has a number of distinctive features (Wright 1999; Milgrom 2000:1327–56; Nihan 2007:545–62). For this reason it was called the Holiness Code (German *Heiligkeitsgesetzt*; often H or HC). The history of its investigation is a classic example of a bold theory that has been progressively reshaped (Hartley 1992:251–60). Originally the majority of this section was understood to be an older, independent collection of laws, which the priestly editors incorporated into their work with only light editing (e.g. the references to Yhwh speaking to Moses). Evidence for the theory included the similarity of H to other collections of law, especially the book of the Covenant (Exod. 20–23) and Deuteronomy 12–28. These begin with a discussion of the place of sacrifice (Lev. 17; Exod. 20:22-26; 25–40; Deut. 12; cf. Ezk. 40) and end with a series of blessings and curses (Lev. 26; Exod. 23:20-33; Deut. 28). In contrast to Leviticus 1–16 there are frequent motive clauses. It has a distinctive vocabulary and style (Driver 1913:49–50; Milgrom 2000:1325–32), especially the repeated 'I am Yhwh', or 'I am Yhwh your God'. It also conveys a distinctive set of theological emphases such as the central place of the land and the summons to the whole people to be holy (Lev. 19:2).

However, Elliger (1966) also argued that H was a later editorial redaction of P, rather than the other way round. This reversal of the direction of dependence was given such a persuasive presentation by the Jewish scholar Israel Knohl that it has now become the new critical orthodoxy. He called the earlier Priestly work Priestly Torah (PT), whereas Leviticus 17 –26 reflects the work of the Holiness School (HS). Rather than being a limited law code, the hand of the HS can be detected at places in P and indeed elsewhere in the Pentateuch. It represents a very late stage in the formation of the Pentateuch (Knohl 1995:104–6). This explains the further influences from the Ten Commandments (Lev. 19), the Covenant Code (Exod. 20:22–23:19) and the Deuteronomic tradition. Knohl argued that Leviticus 17–26 included texts that were dependent on parallels in P (e.g. Lev. 23 draws on Num. 28–29). Knohl also argued, along with other Jewish scholars, that it was largely pre-exilic. Its ethical instruction is strongly influenced by the pre-exilic prophets, who criticized the non-ethical stance of the Priestly writing, represented by Leviticus 1–16. Joosten (1996:203–7) also argued for a pre-exilic date on other grounds, such as its background in a pre-exilic rural milieu, and the portrayal of the resident alien.

One difficulty with Knohl's reconstruction is that the scope of the Holiness School beyond Leviticus 17–27 is disputed. Some attribute fewer texts to it (Milgrom 2000:1343–4; Nihan 2007:569–72). On the other hand Tucker (2017) attributes Pg to the Holiness Composition because of their common language and theology. Others distinguish more redactional stages. Elliger (1966) finds no fewer than four main phases of H, as well as assorted precursors and insertions. Milgrom also finds four strata but also comments that the final H redactor (HR) is merely 'the end product of the H continuum' (2000:1345). Nor were most critical scholars persuaded by Knohl's pre-exilic dating. The dependence of H on P suggests to many that it should be dated to the Persian period. One suggestion is that H represents a synthesis of the extant law codes (especially D and P), perhaps in response to the Persian desire for a unified stance by its sponsored nation.

There is, though, a third approach to the matter, that of the sceptics. Wagner (1974) questioned the existence of the Holiness Code. He pointed to the lack of a coherent order in Leviticus 17–26, in contrast to other Ancient Near Eastern collections of laws. The theme of cultic impurity (11–22) cuts across the traditional division into 11–16 and 17–27. While few have followed his specific analysis, others have emphasized the close relationship between Leviticus 17–27 and the rest of P (Ruwe 1999). Blum (1990:325–29), for example, highlights the significant common theological language of Leviticus 26 and earlier priestly texts (e.g. 'establish/remember the covenant' and 'be fruitful and multiply'). Warning (1999) listed a number of stylistic features (e.g. the number seven) that pervade the whole of the book. Gerstenberger (1996:18) goes so far as to describe the Holiness Code as 'a wishful phantom of scholarly literature'. The main argument for this position is that the differences between H and P are relatively insignificant compared to the differences within these traditions. Furthermore, many of the differences can be explained as arising from different contexts. Scholars who investigate the text in minute detail are likely to emphasize differences that reflect different sources. Those who are more interested in the overall theology and world view work with sufficiently general categories that differences in detail are of relatively little significance in comparison to the overall priestly world view. They are suspicious of the argument from silence, where because P is silent on a particular topic, H is interpreted as holding a different polemical stance.

Although most references to the Holiness Code are to chapters 17–27, some studies refer to 17–26. Leviticus 27 is often described as a later 'Appendix' (Milgrom 2001:2407–9). Although the blessings and curses of Leviticus 26 might be seen as the fitting end for law code, the final chapter avoids closing the book with the curses. It also builds on the Jubilee legislation of Leviticus 25 and continues to explore its theme of redemption. It thus provides another example of the bracketing or chiastic structuring that is found elsewhere in H and P. The discussion reflects the tension between a historical-critical approach that highlights sources or a particular stage of composition, and a literary or canonical approach that works with the final form of the text.

The assumption of this guide is that, while there are differences between the two main parts of Leviticus, there is sufficient overlap of perspective that in most cases it is useful to treat the book as a relatively unified whole. From a thematic point of view Leviticus 17–27 as the second part of the book reflects a movement towards discussion of life in the land rather than matters regarding the sanctuary.

# Leviticus as a book

Turning to literary approaches, there are good reasons to regard Leviticus as a distinct book, rather than being merely part of the larger Priestly writing spanning Exodus, Leviticus and Numbers (Auld 2003). Whereas in Exodus Yhwh calls to Moses from Mount Sinai (Exod. 19:3), at the beginning of Leviticus he calls to him from the Tent of Meeting (Lev. 1:1), which has just been erected (Exod. 35–40). Leviticus ends on Mount Sinai (Lev. 27:34) and includes two summary statements about the giving of the laws to the people (Lev. 26:46; 27:34). On the other hand Numbers opens with Yhwh speaking to Moses in the wilderness of Sinai (Num. 1:1) and is framed by the census accounts of Numbers 1 and 26.

Leviticus is also the central book in the Pentateuch, which can be regarded both as a linear narrative and as a concentric or chiastic structure (ABCBA). Leviticus is the still centre (at Mount Sinai) of a story that begins with the creation of the world and God's people (Genesis) and finishes at the border of the promised land (Deuteronomy). The book of Exodus prepares for the laws of Leviticus in its account of the making of the covenant and the construction and consecration of the Tabernacle. The first part of Numbers begins the preparations for the next stage of the journey (Num. 1:1–10:10).

Genesis and Deuteronomy are the outer wings of the concentric structure and are similar in representing a significant time gap (before and afterwards) from the events described in Exodus, Leviticus and Numbers. There are significant parallels between Exodus and Numbers that set off the time Israel spends at Sinai. Both books include wanderings through the wilderness, the grumbles of Israel and disputes about leadership. Far from being a secondary text, Leviticus may indeed be the theological centre of the entire Pentateuch (Zenger and Frevel 1999:38).

The form of Leviticus also differs subtly from that of the second half of Exodus (Exod. 19–40). The building of the Tabernacle is a one-off founding ritual, whereas the laws of Leviticus imply that they are to be embedded in Israel's ongoing life. They systematically set out a number of possible variations for individual sacrifices and purifications. Although the ordination of Aaron and his sons (Lev. 8–9) and the Day of Atonement (16) tell of their first occurrence, the implication is that they are also patterns for future performance. The laws of Leviticus 17–27 are oriented to life in the land, even though the Israelites remain encamped at Mount Sinai. Leviticus is a complex interweaving of unique narrative and rituals that will be repeated in the future, though not necessarily in precisely the same way.

# The structure of Leviticus

The distinctiveness of the Holiness Code (see above) has led many to find two main divisions in the book: Leviticus 1–16, with a primary cultic emphasis, and 17–27, which treats more general issues of people and land. However, within each division are further subsections that suggest a more nuanced structure. The challenge in determining a structure for Leviticus is that there are several ordering principles evident in the book. The most basic is the divine speech formula, such as the particularly elaborate first verse: 'The LORD summoned Moses and spoke to him from the tent of meeting' (Lev. 1:1). The narrative setting of Leviticus at Mount Sinai is also alluded to at certain points, sometimes linked with the speech formula (Lev. 7:38; 25:1; 26:46; 27:34). However, the distribution of these comments does not indicate a clear middle-level structure. We also need to add the phenomenon of bracketing, the separation of chapters of similar material by one treating a different matter. Thus Leviticus 1 and 3 (animal sacrifices) bracket 2 (cereal offerings), 12 and 15 (impurities of men and women) bracket 13–14 (visible blemishes), 18 and 20 (prohibited sex) bracket 19 (laws of holy living), and 23 and 25 (calendrical laws) bracket 24 (holy things). Yet these do not always indicate a sub-division (e.g. sacrifice is the topic of 1–7, not just 1–3).

It is not surprising, therefore, that scholars have proposed a great number of structures (Luciani 2005). It is tempting to find a sevenfold structure (Hieke 2014:56):

| | | | |
|---|---|---|---|
| A | 1–7 | Sacrifice | |
| | B | 8–10 | Priesthood |
| | | C | 11–15 | Purity and impurity |
| | | | D | 16–17 | Sacrifice and atonement |
| | | C' | 18-20 | Holy behaviour for the people |
| | B' | 21–22 | Holy priestly behaviour |
| A' | 23–27 | Holy time | |

Here Leviticus demonstrates a chiastic or ring-like structures, with later sections echoing earlier ones in reverse. So 8–10 and 21–22 (B-B') address priestly behaviour, while 11–15 and 18–20 treat matters of impurity that affect the people. However, there are alternatives. For example, Milgrom (2000:1364–7), following Douglas (1995:247–55), argues for the centrality of Leviticus 19 in an elaborate ring structure. There do appear to be good arguments for Leviticus 16 to be the central chapter (Rendtorff 2003), as well as bringing to a climax the first part of the book. Indeed, some see this as the heart of the Pentateuch as a whole (Morales 2015:29). Leviticus 17 appears to be more of a transitional chapter and is usually seen as the start of the second half of the book, the Holiness Code.

The value of these proposals is that they highlight certain links between sections and chapters. But it is possible that these links do not point to a coherent concentric structure. A significant problem for all such analyses is that the opening section on sacrifice has relatively little overlap in content or style with the final chapters. The content and style change so much as the book progresses that the reader is more likely to note a linear progression rather than a ring structure (Watts 2013:12–20). As is the case for other biblical books, there is evidence of several structuring principles, but none completely controls the final form of the book.

# The world in front of the text: The purpose of Leviticus

An area of growing interest in biblical criticism is the role of readers, both the original recipients of the text and subsequent readers. Anyone taking the effort to produce a text has some kind of purpose and wishes readers to understand and share its message. There is a rhetorical as well as a literary dimension to Leviticus. So who were these readers and what does Leviticus intend to do to them? One view is that at least the first part (Lev. 1–16) was a manual for priests. However, there is relatively little that would be of interest only to priests (6:8[Heb. 6:1]–7:10; 21:1–22:16), and even these texts contribute to an overall understanding of the priestly system. Most of the initial speech formulas are for Moses to speak to the people or the congregation of Israel (e.g. 1:2; 11:2; 17:2). Leviticus is instruction to both priests and people about how to order worship and life before Yhwh in the land that they are about to possess.

Traditional readers assumed that the laws were carried out according to the text. Historical critics often retained this assumption, while shifting the programmatic purpose to the return from exile, rather than the first entry into the land. P intended to provide a blueprint for renewed worship in Jerusalem following the return. The difficulty with this view is that the Tabernacle is by no means the same as a temple. For Fretheim (1968) this is evidence that P had an anti-temple polemic and desired a return to a movable sanctuary like the Tabernacle. However, the exilic and post-exilic sources give no hint that anything other than a temple was ever contemplated. The relation between P and any specific historical setting (Mosaic, monarchy, exile) remains indirect, disputed and puzzling. Scholarly disagreement reflects the success with which its 'fictional' character (Liss 2006) has concealed its historical origins. This theoretical character has led to it being described as a 'utopian vision' (Knohl 1995:156), although this description does not really fit P's stark recognition of imperfection, impurity and sin.

It may be the case that P never intended to provide a detailed blueprint for a future system of worship. A more flexible approach is indicated by the presence in the Pentateuch of three law codes that differ from one another in their detail (Exod. 21–23; Lev. 17–26; Deut. 12–26). The implication is that the editors of the Pentateuch were aware that laws were illustrative rather than statutory. It was expected that readers would adapt the laws in a contextually appropriate way, while paying careful attention to the principles underlying the particulars (Berman 2017). The purpose of the Priestly writing appears to be pedagogic rather than programmatic. It is Torah, understood as instruction or teaching, rather than law that is meant to be applied according to the letter. We might compare the traditional Jewish curriculum based on the Talmud, which has distant historical roots but is intended to teach ways of thinking that are both innovative and faithful. The purpose of Leviticus would then be to instruct its readers about the basic principles of worship and ethics through a worked example, which might also be an imaginative composite portrait.

In this view Leviticus sets out one model for how worship and life in the land might reflect the character of Israel and its God. Its underlying theology of holiness and obedience are permanently constitutive of Israelite identity but need to be appropriately adapted for other times and places. Although it is no doubt based upon specific practices and laws drawn from sources describing historical practice, it is ultimately a 'thought experiment', similar to that found in Ezekiel 40–48 (Haran 2008) or the Temple Scroll (11QT) from Qumran. There may be only a loose connection between a ritual text and its actual practice (Wright 2012). If this is the case, then there is little point to the search for one specific historical setting. A more fitting approach would be to understand how the Leviticus seeks to integrate theology, worship and ethics. 'The primary message of Leviticus seems to have been theological' (Grabbe 2003:222), with little interest in informing us about its relation to any historical reality.

Leviticus is primarily a book of law, setting out what Yhwh requires of Israel both in worship and in ordinary life. Like all texts it is intended to communicate to its readers and influence their lives. A major form for this purpose is the description of various ritual practices. These are meant to shape those who engage with them, whether through bodily performance or rehearsal in the imagination. Watts (2007) argues that Leviticus should not be read as a dull handbook for liturgical specialists or as a dangerous excuse for empty ritual. Rather, the frequent repetitions in the laws highlight what is important and invite an attentive response from the hearers and readers.

# Evaluating Leviticus

The previous section emphasized that Leviticus has designs on its readers and expected them to respond wholeheartedly. However, real readers are not passive recipients but react in ways informed by their own beliefs and historical setting. Historical criticism is often associated with a model of scholarship that is cool, objective and neutral. The story of the interpretation of Leviticus demonstrates that it is rarely possible or even interesting to adhere to this ideal. Wellhausen's remarks on P included strong negative judgements about its worth. Its repetitive style reflected 'indescribable pedantry', and its content consisted of 'monstrous growths of legislative matter' (Wellhausen 1885:350, 342). The artistry and genre of the J narrative was the paradigm against which P fell grievously short.

Wellhausen's criticisms were linked to a grand narrative of the origin, rise and fall of Israelite religion. In the nineteenth century the prophets were the key representatives of authentic Israelite faith, emphasizing the free, natural response of individuals to the one God. A key move in the documentary hypothesis was to date the prophets before the law, which was developed in exilic and post-exilic times. P lost touch with the roots of Israelite faith and instead constructed an artificial Judaism based on law. This reconstruction is now generally regarded as oversimplistic. While the extensive collections of law are no longer dated back to Moses, the prophets did indeed assume some kind of law (Zimmerli 1965). Wellhausen's evaluation of law reflects Germany's liberal Protestant heritage. This included an emphasis on grace at the expense of law and was especially suspicious of ritualistic forms of religion. Koehler (1957:181) even described the Israelite cult as 'man's expedient for his own redemption'.

The Protestant suspicion of law and ritual has been effectively reversed in more recent scholarship. Willis (2009:xviii) has even suggested that P might be seen as the 'ever after' phase of a romantic love story. The drama of the Exodus, with its climax in the making of the covenant (Exod. 19; 24), may excite us most, but the 'routine tasks, such as maintaining the house (the sanctuary) and doing the laundry (purification laws)', are vital skills for ensuring that the relationship continues to flourish. Yhwh graciously provides the means by which Israel is able to respond to his salvation. Ritual studies (e.g. Bell 1992) have emphasized that belief and ethics are more than an intellectual matter and that lives are powerfully shaped by the participation of the body and the senses in repeated ritual actions. The many-sided and complex nature of ritual also allows participants to interpret its meaning in different ways, and the significance of a ritual can evolve over time in response to new contexts.

Reception criticism, the exploration of the interpretation of the Bible throughout history, is of growing interest. Theologians and commentators were often creative in going beyond the text for the sake of finding a relevant word for today. Yet the status of Leviticus as Holy Scripture also required them to take the text seriously and ensure that even though they went beyond it, they did not go against it. This respect and limitation is no longer necessarily the case for those who approach the text from another faith or world view. A growing number of volumes seek to evaluate the book from a committed stance that questions the ethics and theology of the text (e.g. from a feminist, sociological or post-colonial perspective).

# The characteristics of this guide

Interpreting a text has been compared to how we might look at a stained glass window (Clines 1997:12). We can ask about the world behind the window (the historical approach), although our lack of knowledge about the authors of Leviticus makes this a tentative enterprise. Alternatively we can analyse the picture before us and seek to grasp its artistry and content as fully as we can (the literary approach). Or we can ask how the window might have influenced the lives of its intended viewers, for better or for worse. And because the complex and richly coloured book of Leviticus comes from a distant country that we know little about, it is fitting for its viewers to approach it with patience and imagination.

The goal of this guide is to introduce the larger questions and issues that Leviticus raises for its readers. It will note some of the historical-critical discussion about the sources and setting of the book, but my skepticism about many of the results will be evident. Instead, more emphasis will be placed on the final form of the book. It will argue that Leviticus reflects a largely coherent conception of the world, whatever its origins. Much of the interest in the book is its descriptive character. This has required scholars to go beyond the text and construct syntheses that are imaginative and contestable rather than proven. This has also highlighted how the world view of readers shapes their interpretation, especially when the topics addressed are alien to the culture of the day or strongly disputed. So each chapter includes reflection on the assumptions that modern readers bring to the text.

# 2

# Holiness

## Key Priestly concepts

Before we consider the main sections of Leviticus it is helpful to explore some of the key concepts that underlie many of the detailed laws and are at the heart of the Priestly world view. Indeed, the subtitle of this guide suggests that one particular concept dominates all others: holiness. Milgrom (2000:1397) states simply that 'the theme of the entire book of Leviticus is holiness'. This echoes the theological traditions that regard holiness as a central category in discussing the character and nature of divinity. On the other hand the meaning of holiness is by no means clear, and many regard its different nuances as an indication of the disunity of Leviticus more than its coherence.

Scholars range on a spectrum from those who regard the Levitical concept of holiness as a coherent and complex whole and those who find in it various distinct traditions that reflect different historical settings and theologies. The great majority of historical-critical scholars follow the second approach, so the presentation below reflects a minority report. Whichever view is held, the need to maintain and encourage holiness drives much of Leviticus. Since holiness is incompatible with impurity, the appropriate rituals of purification are vital (ch. 5). The threat to holiness from sin and impurity is dealt with by the mandatory sacrifices (ch. 3), and it is also the reason for the climactic ritual of the Day of Atonement (ch. 7). The requirement for the people to be holy in an appropriate way for them becomes prominent in the second part of Leviticus (ch. 6). Holiness also characterizes holy time, which by its nature is not bound closely to a specific place, but nonetheless characterizes various days and seasons that are dedicated to Yhwh in a special way (ch. 7).

From a semantic point of view holiness is closely related to several other important priestly terms. Moses instructs the priests to 'distinguish between the holy (*qōḏeš*) and the common (*ḥōl*), and between the unclean (*ṭāmēʾ*) and the clean (*ṭāhôr*)' (Lev. 10:10). The frequent occurrence of these in Leviticus and elsewhere is often lost in English translation. 'Sacred' sometimes translates holy items (e.g. priestly clothing), even though it is unhelpful to put these into a different category. The related verb can be rendered as 'sanctify', 'consecrate' or 'hallow'. 'Clean' and 'unclean' tend to evoke a modern hygienic notion of cleanliness, so translators often prefer 'purity' and 'impurity', or 'purify' and 'defile' for the corresponding verb. These indicate more clearly the ritual and symbolic significance of these terms, although it is customary to refer to clean and unclean creatures (Lev. 11). The noun translated 'common' or 'profane' only occurs in Leviticus in the verse cited and is a neutral term. The related verb usually has a strong negative character since it describes a deliberate crossing of boundaries that should be kept distinct.

Leviticus 10:10 lists two related pairs. The realm of the holy is distinct from that of the common, which consists of the further mutually exclusive pair, the pure and the impure. Many of the rituals in Leviticus describe movements between these states. The following is a useful summary, though such diagrams always run the risk of oversimplification (Figure 1) (Wenham 1979:19; Hieke 2014:124–6).

Purity is the 'neutral' midway point or buffer zone between holiness and impurity, which must never come into contact. If this did happen, it would lead to a holy-impure 'fusion reaction' that would threaten the integrity of the whole system (Nelson 1993:33–6). The careful organization of the Tabernacle is designed to prevent this, as well as all the laws for how ritual is to be properly conducted. When Aaron's two sons offered 'strange fire' (Lev. 10:1-2), a divine fiery judgement ensured that the integrity of the sanctuary was preserved. A lay Israelite had to be pure before approaching and

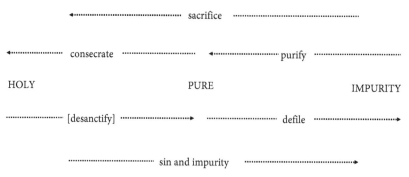

**Figure 1** The dynamic priestly system of sanctification and defilement

entering the sanctuary (12:4), and this was especially vital for priests. Aaron and his sons had to be purified before they were consecrated (8:6) and had to purify themselves in order to minister within the sanctuary (Exod. 30:19-21). When priests left the sanctuary, they lost their active holiness, since they can then incur physical impurity without blame (Lev. 21:1-4). Although Leviticus does not have any terminology for this (hence the brackets in the diagram above), it can be called desanctification. Similar desanctification from a stage of extreme holiness occurred when the High Priest completed his work in the Holy of Holies on the Day of Atonement and washed his clothes (16:23-24). The holiness of metal vessels used for cooking holy meat can be nullified by boiling, scouring and rinsing, rather than being broken as for clay vessels (6:28 [Heb. 21]). When the verb 'profane' is used, it refers to deliberate actions intended to compromise the holy, such as not keeping the Sabbath (Exod. 31:14) or swearing falsely by Yhwh's name (Lev. 19:12). Certain weighty sins led to a form of major impurity that profaned Yhwh's holy name and defiled the sanctuary (18:21; 20:3).

# The meaning of holiness

There have been numerous attempts to define holiness (Budd 1989; Jenson 2003). Discerning which of these makes the best sense in Leviticus is complex, because of the frequency of its occurrence (some 143 times) and its range of reference. Leviticus refers to holy places, holy things, holy priests, holy people, and holy living, and it is also defined by its relation to purity and impurity. How much consistency there is in these different associations of holiness has been a lively topic of debate. Because conclusions often depend on how holiness is defined, it will help to review some of the different approaches.

1 Holiness as experience of the divine. The influential book by Otto, *The Idea of the Holy* (1959, first published in German in 1917), emphasized the terrifying yet compelling feeling that arose from an encounter with the holy, the mysterious divine other (*mysterium tremendum et fascinans*). However, the focus on dramatic encounters (e.g. Isa. 6) tends to highlight the exceptional and the occasional at the expense of the regular and the normal. Yhwh does respond when the holy sanctuary is threatened (Lev. 10:1-2), but the purpose of the architecture of the Tabernacle and the laws of Leviticus was

to encourage a conscious but safe encounter with the holy God as a steady source of life and blessing. This purpose of the Tabernacle is highlighted by its other name, the Tent of Meeting (Exod. 29:43-46). The Priestly ritual system enables the people to enter the presence of the holy Lord and so receive his forgiveness and blessing. This is a physical and social event. In Leviticus there is little emphasis on the individual experience, perhaps because the Israelites had as wide a range of personal response to approaching God as people have today. The modern notion of interiority and sense of the inner presence of God is also distant from the text (Taylor 1989:111–98).

2   Holiness as the distinctive attribute of God. Theologians sometimes define holiness as the essential 'godness' of God. Holiness is the nearest we have to a completely unique category, whereas elsewhere we speak of God in metaphoric language that has a human or earthly equivalent (e.g. jealous, righteous). Yet while the biblical texts emphasize that God is supremely holy and the source of all holiness, that holiness is expressed on earth through a carefully structured set of objects and laws. The ritual of the consecration of the first priests (Exod. 40:12-13; Lev. 8–9) relates holiness to many aspects of human life. Even though holiness communicates a clear sense of transcendence and otherness, this is not an irrational or incomprehensible 'wholly other'.

3   Holiness as separation. Leviticus 10:10 tells the priests to 'distinguish between the holy and the common, and between the unclean and the clean'. 'Distinguish' here represents the verb often translated 'separate' (e.g. Gen. 1:4). But while the consecration of a temple or a priest separates from the realm of the common, this is a consequence of holiness rather than its essence. Holiness refers to a positive rather than a negative quality. Consecration inevitably involves a separation *from*, but the primary goal is a separation *for* or *to* Yhwh (Exod. 35:2; Lev. 20:26; 21:6-7).

4   Holiness as wholeness. The anthropologist Mary Douglas suggested that 'to be holy is to be whole, to be one; holiness is unity, integrity, perfection of the individual and the kind' (Douglas 1966:6). Thus priests and sacrificial animals have to be unblemished (Lev. 21:17-23; 22:17-25) and the people are forbidden to use certain mixtures (19:19). However, the two concepts are not identical (Olyan 2008). Blemished priests may still eat of most holy food (v. 22), and some kinds of mixtures are holy (see ch. 7 on Lev. 19). 'Wholeness' is perhaps too abstract and unnuanced a concept to capture the central meaning of holiness.

5  Holiness as belonging to God. Holiness is perhaps best understood as simply that which belongs to a god in a special way. When something became holy in Israel, it became part of Yhwh's sphere or realm (Joosten 1996:124) and is consequently subject to special laws that do not apply to that which is not holy. The clearest metaphor for this is spatial. Yhwh manifests himself on Mount Sinai, which has to be kept holy (Exod. 19:23) and so separated from other regions. The Tabernacle is a portable Sinai, and its detailed description (25–31; 35–40) provides an essential orientation to Leviticus's understanding of holiness and how the rituals and behaviour can maintain its holiness despite impurity and sin.

# The Tabernacle

There is a close association between holiness and God's presence. The goal of the covenant is Yhwh's dwelling in the midst of his people: 'Have them make me a sanctuary (*miqdāš*), so that I may dwell (*škn*) among them' (Exod. 25:8). The verb 'dwell' is the source of the noun translated 'Tabernacle' (*miškān*). Yhwh dwells first of all in his holy palace or temple in heaven (Ps. 11:4). The earthly Tabernacle shares this holiness through correspondence (Exod. 25:9) and consecration (40:9) so is able to mediate the divine presence and glory (40:34-35). However, for human beings closeness to God is dangerous, since even to see God is to die (Gen. 32:30; Judg. 13:22). Holiness is incompatible with the transience and impurity that characterizes earthly human life. The Tabernacle is therefore as carefully constructed as a nuclear reactor. There are a series of barriers and spaces that moderate God's holiness in a graduated way and are correlated with different kinds of sacrifice impurity (see ch. 5) (Figure 2).

The gradation is partially conveyed by the vocabulary of holiness (Jenson 1992:89–93; Hundley 2013). The innermost part of the Tabernacle, the inner sanctuary, is called the Holy of Holies, a Hebrew idiom for the superlative (i.e. the most holy place). It contains the ark of the covenant, over which reside the cherubim who support the throne of God (Exod. 25:22). A curtain or veil (26:33) separates it from the next section, the outer sanctuary (25:23-40). This is often called the Holy Place and contains the golden altar of incense, the table for the bread of the presence and the golden lampstand (the Menorah). All these are divine counterparts of the essential furniture of a royal palace, addressing the senses of smell, taste and sight, and are

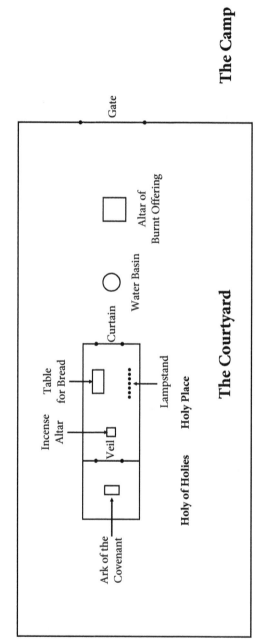

**Figure 2** The Tabernacle

**Figure 3** The Holiness Spectrum

|          | Most holy | Holy | Pure | Impure | Most impure |
|----------|-----------|------|------|--------|-------------|
| *Spatial* | Holy of Holies inner sanctuary | Holy Place outer sanctuary | courtyard, camp | camp | outside the camp |
| *Personal* | High Priest | priests | Levites, Israelites | minor impurities | major impurities |
| *Ritual* | sacrifice | sacrifice | sacrifice | minor purification | major purification |
| *Temporal* | Day of Atonement | festivals, Sabbath | common days | | |

incorporated into various priestly rituals. The courtyard outside includes areas of different holiness, ranging from the most holy altar of sacrifice (29:37) to areas where ordinary Israelites can gather. The main purpose of the various barriers and entrances is to protect the holy areas from defilement by anything impure.

The spatial graduation can also be extended outwards. Minor impurity and temporary major impurity (e.g. menstruation) are tolerated within the camp, but more permanent major impurities, such as those with scale disease, belong outside the camp, in the wilderness (Lev. 13:46; see further ch. 4). These spatial gradations can be partly coordinated with the primary features of the cult, including people, ritual and time. So long as it is not taken too rigidly it can be helpful to align the different categories in what may be called the Holiness Spectrum (Figure 3) (Jenson 1992).

These are impressively coordinated on the Day of Atonement, the only time when the High Priest enters the Holy of Holies and offers sacrifice for his own sins and for that of the nation (Lev. 16).

# Two kinds of holiness

In the schema introduced in the last section the holiness of the sanctuary is coordinated with the holiness of the priests, who are restricted to the priestly family of Aaron. This enables them to serve in the sanctuary. However, other texts in Leviticus describe the whole people of Israel as being holy. This general kind of holiness is the purpose of the food laws (Lev. 11:44-45) and at the heart of the dramatic call to all in Leviticus 19:2 ('You shall be holy, for I, Yhwh your God, am holy').

Historical-critical approaches usually assign the more restricted idea of holiness to P and the more general to H. The opinions about why this is so vary wildly. At one end it indicates a strong corrective intention. Kugler (1997:26) highlights the tension in suggesting that 'Leviticus is a book at war within itself theologically'. On the other hand, Crüsemann (1996:278) highlights continuity in stating that H 'is no foreign body in the context. ... there are no real contradictions'. In the present form of Leviticus there is no explicit sign that the final redactors found a serious contradiction between the different parts of the book. Nihan (2007:546) acknowledges the speculative character of the views that propose an underlying model of conflict when he comments that Leviticus 17–26 'apparently' seeks to correct or revise P.

One reason for finding limited discontinuity is that H maintains a strong emphasis on the distinctiveness of priestly holiness, especially in Leviticus 20–21. Yhwh sanctifies the priests (21:15, 23; 22:9,16) as well as the people (Lev. 20:8; 22:32). It is possible to see here a later extension of an earlier Priestly idea of restricted cultic holiness, but it may reflect a complementary rather than a revisionist approach. There may well be historical development, but a good case can be made for continuity rather than contradiction. Thus Wright (1999:363) suggests that 'while the Holiness School does not revolutionize the Priestly Torah tradition, it explains, adapts, updates, and reformulates it'.

There are various reasons why scholars have found divergence between H and P. For Knohl the Priestly Torah 'has a ritual character devoid of any moral content' (Knohl 1995:151). The Holiness School was influenced by the eighth-century prophets, who sharply criticized cultic practice that ignored social justice (e.g. Isa. 1:10-17; Amos 2:6-16), a theme conspicuously absent in P. In contrast, Leviticus 17–26 teach that 'the concept of holiness also encompasses the realm of social justice' (Knohl 1990:180). However, the final form of Leviticus holds together both cult and ethics, and the tension between them may betray modern assumptions (Cothey 2005; Trevaskis 2011). We would expect distinct emphases in texts that differ in genre and purpose. In Leviticus 1–16 the main concerns are the sanctuary and how to deal with the impurity that threatens its holiness. We would not necessarily expect significant ethical comment in a cultic text, and there are a few texts that do refer to the moral realm (e.g. Lev. 6:1-7 [Heb. 5:20-26]; 16:21). Furthermore, it is unlikely that the Priestly writers were so out of step with the foundational requirements of the covenant, especially if the documents are dated late.

Another suggestion is that P represents a static notion of holiness, whereas that of H is dynamic (Wright 1999; Milgrom 2000:1718–20; Schwartz 2000; Regev 2001). In P holiness pre-exists as a status, whereas in H holiness is required and the people have to achieve it through keeping the commandments. But again there may be contextual reasons for the differences. The static character of P is in large part because the sanctuary is a stable construction that does not need to maintain its holiness in the same way that people need to. If that holiness is threatened by human action, then divine sanction follows (Lev. 10:1-3). In H the emphasis is on the ongoing behaviour of the people in areas of life that require guidance and regulation. But this also assumes that there is a pre-existing covenantal status that is the basis for instruction (Lev. 19:36; 20:26). Both parts of Leviticus assume a status (the 'static') that has to be maintained (the 'dynamic'). The holiness of God is a disposition or attribute that does not need to be defined by a particular action, just as glass remains fragile even if it is not broken (Sonderegger 2015:487).

The section Leviticus 1–16 also includes some texts that refer to general holiness (e.g. Lev. 11:44-45). It is possible to assign references to general holiness in Leviticus 1–16 to H, but there is a danger of a circular argument. Even if such texts are later redactional additions, then this would suggest differences between the ideologies of P and H may be less than has been often assumed. There is a narrative and logical narrative in the way that the first part of Leviticus focuses more on sanctuary matters, whereas 17–27 opens out to how the people are to behave towards each other and the land. The distinctiveness of H's view has sometimes been traced to the influence of Deuteronomy, which also emphasizes the holiness of the people (Deut. 7:8; 28:9). However, H develops various themes in its own way which is distinct from Deuteronomy, suggesting that simple linear schemes of influence (P, then Dt, then H) are oversimplifications (Rhyder 2019).

It is also possible to incorporate priestly and general holiness within a more comprehensive idea of holiness. This has been anticipated by the opening definition of holiness as that which belongs to God in a special way. Holiness can therefore vary depending on whether the context is internal to Israel (priests are holy in contrast to non-priests) or external (Israel is holy as a people in contrast to other nations). The subject matter of the book of Leviticus accounts for the different emphases in the two main halves of the book. Leviticus 1–16 sets out the distinctive character of the Tabernacle and its rituals so that the distinctions between priests and non-priests are highlighted. Leviticus 17–27 is more concerned with the identity of Israel as a whole and its distinctiveness compared to the nations. The general holiness of Lev. 11:44-45 may not be so exceptional, since the entire chapter concerns the behaviour of the people, not just priests. When Leviticus 17–27 discusses priests and the High Priest, it reflects graded cultic holiness.

This contextual approach can stand alongside a source-critical approach, in that a redactor could have combined the sources into the book we now have. But at some point the necessity for identifying strongly distinct sources is called into question. There are striking developments, and even contradictions, in the various priestly traditions embedded in Exodus, Leviticus and Numbers. However, what may be more significant, especially from a theological point of view, is the overall coherence. The differences represent the contextual working out of a consistent priestly logic and grammar (Meshel 2014).

This approach is consistent with a canonical approach to the final text. The people of Israel belong to God in a special way, since through covenant they become 'a priestly kingdom and a holy nation' (Exod. 19:6). This is taken up in those parts of Leviticus that emphasize general holiness (especially Lev. 17–26). The cult and its priestly servants have a subordinate role within this overall vision of a holy people. This is consistent with the frequent references to the people of Israel in Leviticus 1–16. Because they serve in the sanctuary priests too have to be consecrated and so attain the same holy status (Lev. 8:12, 30), but their primary role is to ensure the ongoing purity and well-being of the people.

# 3

# Sacrifice (Leviticus 1–7)

## The structure of Leviticus 1–7

The book of Exodus ends with an account of the building and the consecration of the Tabernacle (Exod. 35–40), which enables Yhwh to dwell in the midst of his people (25:8). However, this is only possible if the relationship between Yhwh and his people is maintained, and Leviticus begins with main way this happens, sacrifice (Anderson 1987; Averbeck 2003; Marx 2005). Through sacrifice sin and impurity are dealt with, and life-giving communication between God and his people is opened up. Although the instructions about sacrifice are generic, the divine speech formula and especially the conclusion (7:38) set them within the account of the revelation at Sinai.

Leviticus 1–7 is divided into two sections, each of them covering the main kinds of sacrifice. The first addresses the people of Israel, whereas the second refers to details of main interest to the priests, although the people of Israel are included in the address (7:23, 29).

| | | |
|---|---|---|
| 1:1-2 | Introduction | |
| 1–5 | The individual sacrifices and offerings | |
| 1–3 | Voluntary offerings | |
| 1 | Burnt offering | |
| 2 | Grain offering | |
| 3 | Well-being offering | |
| 4–5 | Required offerings | |
| 4 | Purification offering | |
| 5:1-13 | Purification offering: scaled | |
| 5:14–6:7 [Heb. 5:14-26] | Reparation offering | |
| 6:8–7:34 | Laws of the sacrifices and offerings | |
| 6:8-13 [Heb. 6:1-6] | Law of the burnt offering | |
| 6:14-18 [Heb. 6:7-11] | Law of the grain offering | |
| 6:19-23 [Heb. 6:12-16] | Offering at the anointing of the priests | |

| | |
|---|---|
| 6:24-30 [Heb. 6:17-23] | Law of the purification offering |
| 7:1-10 | Law of the reparation offering |
| 7:11-18 | Law of the well-being offering |
| 7:19-34 | Miscellaneous instructions |

7:35-38    Conclusion

The order of the voluntary sacrifices in the first section is probably related to their divine orientation. The burnt offering is totally devoted to Yhwh, the grain offering is shared by Yhwh and the priests (and often accompanies the burnt offering), while the majority of the well-being offering is eaten by the offeror. Sacrifices that are required in certain circumstances are then treated. The purification offering deals with serious impurity and inadvertent sin, while the closely related reparation offering is for those who have defrauded others.

Non-Priestly texts indicate a twofold distinction between burnt offerings (ʿolot) and either sacrifices (zᵉḇāḥim) or well-being offerings (šᵉlāmim). They do not mention the purification offering and reparation offering, probably because these are specific sacrifices that relate to the purification of the Temple/Tabernacle (Milgrom 1991:176). The non-Priestly burnt offering probably covers their role in dealing with sin. There is a fundamental distinction between sacrifices that lead to a celebratory meat meal (well-being offerings) and all others that relate primarily to Yhwh.

A ritual may include two or more sacrifices, and the order of their performance differs from the order listed in Leviticus 1–5 (Rainey 1970). For example, the final stage of the restoration of the person with skin disease (Lev. 14:12-20) begins with the reparation and purification offerings, probably because these atoning sacrifices deal with the impurity that separates Yhwh and the offeror. A burnt offering then confirms the offeror ability to relate directly to Yhwh, perhaps with overtones of praise and obedience. Finally the well-being offering widens the circle of celebration to include the offeror's family and confirms the resumption of normal life.

A sacrifice usually calls for the slaughter of an animal and a complex accompanying ritual. However, there are also non-animal objects that are dedicated to God, such as the grain offering (Lev. 2:1), the flour of the purification offering for the poor (5:11), the first fruits of the grain harvest (23:14), and precious metals (Num. 7:13). All these are called *qorbān*, generally translated 'offering'. It derives from the verb 'to draw near' (*qrb*), and the verb and noun are combined in the phrase 'to bring near an offering' (Lev. 1:2; 'to present a present', Watts 2013:181). A physical movement into the realm and presence of Yhwh is central to the character of sacrifices and offerings in the Priestly system.

# The diversity of sacrifice

All cultures develop ways of communicating with the realm of the divine. The precise form depends on the conception of the god, the materials available and the purpose of the communication. In the ancient world it was assumed that the most costly and effective form of communication was sacrifice. However, these assumptions no longer hold in the modern world, and the lack of any clear rationale surrounds the phenomenon with mystery, evident in Geller's lament (1992:99), 'His motto seems to be, "Never explain!"'. There are a number of key interpretive terms, but their significance is generally open and ambiguous, rather than parts of a unified system. The interpretive challenge is heightened by how the meaning of sacrifice has changed radically over time, in response to changing circumstances.

One response to this variety (or chaos) has been to uncover a theoretical master key that unlocks its central mystery (see the next section). However, it is more helpful to treat sacrifice flexibly. It is more like a language or a toolbox that can be adapted for a vast range of purposes than a single sentence with a definite meaning. We might compare the many different forms that the Eucharist or Mass can take and the multiple purposes a particular performance can fulfil. The basic elements of sacrifice can be compared to words. These are put together in sentences (a particular sacrifice), which can then be combined into a larger discourse (a multi-element ritual). The possibilities are, however, constrained by certain rules comparable to grammar. A sacrificial grammar guides the way a specific sacrificial ritual combines animals, objects, people and actions for a particular purpose (Meshel 2014).

Some of the choices available in a sacrificial ritual include the following:

- animal: kind (animal/bird, male/female, goat/sheep/bull), age (young/old), and number
- personnel: the officiant (priest/High Priest), the offeror (priest, elder, ordinary person)
- purpose: corrective (dealing with impurity or sin), transitional (ordination of a priest, reincorporation of someone with skin disease), social (enjoying a meal in God's presence)
- blood: how manipulated (sprinkled, applied, poured out), and where (the Holy of Holies, the Holy Place, the sacrificial altar)
- timing: occasional, weekly, monthly, annual
- other: flowing water, hyssop, scapegoat

The typical plot of a sacrifice included six stages, with the layperson performing 1-3 and the priest 4-6.

1 Presentation. An unblemished animal is brought to the sanctuary. The cost reflects the seriousness of the reason for sacrifice and the commitment of the person offering.
2 Hand-laying. The offeror lays a hand on the head of the animal. This indicated the representative and (according to some) the substitutionary role of the animal.
3 Slaughter. It is slaughtered at the entrance of the Tabernacle and cut up.
4 Blood manipulation. The priests perform a blood ritual.
5 Part or all of the sacrifice is burned.
6 Parts of the sacrifice may be given to the priest and to the offeror for distribution to their family and others.

The descriptive nature of the text leaves room for a wide range of explanations. Some aspects of sacrifice may simply be traditional or practically necessary. A sacrifice may foreground a certain stage of the action and background others. Thus the well-being offerings highlight stage 6, the opportunity to eat meat, while the blood manipulation of stage 4 is central to a purification or reparation offering. Eberhart (2004) highlights stage 5, which is common to all the sacrifices and the climax of the communication between the people on earth and the God of heaven.

# Essentialist theories of sacrifice

A number of attempts have been made to discern the essence or heart or original meaning of sacrifice. These often focus on one or more of the stages of sacrifice set out in the previous section.

1 Sacrifice as food for the god (stage 6). The general analogy of the temple to a palace or house fits the idea of the sacrifice as food provided for the god by his servants (Lev. 21:17, 22). In Mesopotamia the central role of the priests was the 'care and feeding of the gods' in the temple (Oppenheim 1977:183–97). While often dismissed as 'fossilized vestiges' (Milgrom 1991:440), the ancients understand well enough that gods did not eat or drink in the same way as human beings. This view is only found in polemical satires such as the apocryphal Bel and

the Dragon, where Daniel helps the Babylonian king discover that the servants of Bel are secretly eating the offerings. Food is an important social and covenantal symbol, and the significance of sharing food is embedded in some of Israel's central theological texts (Gen. 18; Exod. 24:11). This dimension is prominent in the well-being offering (Lev. 3:11, 16), and the priests offer the 'food of their God' (21:6). The metaphoric character of this symbolism is little different from the invocation of the sense of smell in describing the 'pleasing odour' of a sacrifice (1:9). What matters is what it communicates: the material reality of the covenantal relationship between Yhwh and the people.

2  Sacrifice as the channelling of human violence onto a sacrificial victim (stages 3, 4). Two very influential theoreticians of sacrifice are Girard (1972) and Burkert (1983). They both emphasize the violent propensity of human nature that is channelled and defused by the sacrifice of a victim. However, these theories presuppose a highly speculative history of sacrifice and provide little insight into the language and theology of Priestly sacrifice (Klawans 2006:22–7).

3  Sacrifice as a defence against hostile demonic powers (stage 4). Milgrom (1991:257) traces the origin of impurity to an air-borne demonic power: 'For both Israel and her neigbors impurity was a physical substance, an aerial miasma that possessed magnetic attraction for the realm of the sacred.' Sacrificial blood served an apotropaic purpose (i.e. turns away evil), ensuring that these powers did not prevail. However, the Israelite doctrines of monotheism and human sinfulness led to the transformation of the concept by P into a sign of human responsibility and sin. It is humans, not demons, who are the source of impurity and are the reason why the sanctuary has to be purified. Milgrom (1976) vividly drew on Oscar Wilde's novel, *The Picture of Dorian Gray*, in which the central character's depraved way of life affects his picture rather than his person. Similarly human impurity affects the sanctuary, not the person. The blood of the purification offering deals with the sanctuary, while the impure person is purified through washing (Lev. 15:13, 28) and forgiven because of his remorse. The main difficulty with this proposal is that it assumes a development in the history of sacrifice for which there is little evidence. The texts also indicate that it is the person as well as the sanctuary that needs to be purified (Kiuchi 1987:59–62). There is a close correlation between atonement and forgiveness (4:26). The sacrificial ritual inevitably takes part in different stages but constitutes a unity. Sin and impurity are

bound together both in the sinful action and in the remedy provided by the sacrificial ritual.

4 Sacrifice as the substitutionary death of an animal for a sinner (stages 2–4). The death of the animal substitutes for the death that a sinner deserves, because of God's righteous judgement on sin. However, the focus of the sacrifices translated 'sin offering' is more likely to be purification (see below). The ritual of sacrifice also includes far more than simple substitution. When an offeror lays a hand on the sacrificial animal, there is as much identification and representation as substitution. This theory is particularly attractive to Christians, who understand the sacrificial death of Christ in terms of the sin offering (e.g. Rom. 3:25). However, the reference to the death of Christ as a sacrifice requires a complex conversation between interpretive frameworks that belong to significantly different cultures and contexts.

5 Sacrifice as a gift from the offeror to the god (stage 1). This is a generalization of the previous theory and implied by several sacrificial terms. The grain offering (*minḥâ*, Lev. 2:1) can mean gift or present or tribute in non-Priestly texts (Gen. 32:13; Judg. 3:15). Some early theories regarded this as a commercial exchange, *do-ut-des* ('I give in order that you give'). Offerors give a sacrifice to the deity in order that they might receive blessing or forgiveness. But Leviticus is clear that all that Israel possesses is first of all a gift of grace by Yhwh to his people. The larger narrative context of Leviticus is Yhwh's gracious redemption of Israel, followed by instruction about how they can respond to him in appropriate ways. Anthropologists have emphasized that the receiving and giving of gifts can be an important way of maintaining and developing a relationship of dependence and trust. Indeed, the entire sacrificial system is a gracious gift to Israel revealed to Moses. One problem with the theory is that 'gift' remains a very general and abstract concept. Attempts to be more specific about the nature of the gift, such as homage or thanksgiving, do not do justice to the range of sacrifices.

6 Sacrifice as purification from impurity (stage 4). The incompatibility between holiness and impurity (ch. 2) emphasizes the importance of this function. The basic metaphor is that of water cleansing dirt, and indeed water and time are all that is needed for lesser ritual impurities (ch. 5). But more serious impurities are like deep stains that can only be dealt with by strong detergent or soap. The most powerful means of purification in the priestly system is sacrificial blood, which emphasizes the seriousness of the problem and the cost of its solution. The main

sacrifice for purification is traditionally translated 'sin offering', since it is the same word as 'sin'. However, it often deals with ritual impurities that are not the result of sin and so many scholars prefer to call it 'purification offering' (Milgrom 1991:253–8).

7  Sacrifice as an indication of social status (stages 4, 6). Gilders (2004:181–91) draws on a distinction between the manifest functions of an action (e.g. sacrifice atones) and the latent functions, which are implicit. One important latent function is that the sacrificial system establishes sociocultural distinctions (Nihan 2015), since it legitimates and embeds the status and privileges of the Aaronic priests over against the people. However, it is uncertain how far theories about latent functions say more about the interpreters than the text being interpreted. In the text the priests are no less subordinate to the divine command than the people.

All of these approaches highlight some features of sacrifice and downplay others. Interpreting sacrifice also involves the world of the reader and the world of the text. The opacity and multivalence of sacrifice always require interpreters to move beyond the strict letter of the text in a creative way, which can limit as much as illuminate. One general observation is that the less a theory pays attention to the terminology and practice of Leviticus, the more likely it is to reduce the meaning of sacrifice to that which resonates with the world of the interpreter.

# The burnt offering (Lev. 1; 6:8-13 [Heb. 6:1-6])

Moving to a consideration of the individual sacrifices, the first listed is the burnt offering (ʿōlāh). The Hebrew noun is derived from a verb meaning to go up, probably referring to the ascending smoke or smell of the sacrifice. Watts (2013) therefore calls it the rising offering, but because its distinctive feature is that all of it is burnt, it is usually called the burnt offering or whole offering. While the hide is given to the priest (Lev. 7:8), this does not affect the emphasis that this is a costly act, where the offeror gains no benefit and the priest does not receive any portion of meat. The democratic and gracious character of sacrifice is emphasized by the cheapest offering (a bird) being as acceptable as the most expensive.

The purpose of the ritual appears to be indicated by Lev. 1:4: 'as atonement for you' (NRSV; see below on this term). However, elsewhere it is the purification offering rather than the burnt offering that atones. One suggestion is that this association derives from an earlier period, before the burnt offering was distinguished from the purification offering. Or atonement might be always required because of the danger of approaching God (Levine 1989:6–7). Or the note about atonement may be an addition that reflects the increased importance of the need for atonement in the exilic and post-exilic eras. Or it may be unnecessary to set up strict boundaries between the functions of the sacrifices, since all of them involved blood, the major atoning element. There could thus be an overlap between the purposes of the burnt offering and the purification offering. Finally, the burnt offering can also be regarded as a general-purpose sacrifice, answering 'every conceivable emotional and psychological need' (Milgrom 1991:176).

Nevertheless, the burnt offering has a specifically divine orientation. It is more like a psalm of praise than a plea or lament. The giving up of a costly animal is a fitting honouring and acknowledgement of the unique God of Israel. In turn, Yhwh graciously accepts the sacrifice as a representation of the offeror's devotion, expressed in terms of the sacrifice being 'an offering by fire (ʾiššê) of pleasing aroma (rēaḥ nihōaḥ) to Yhwh'. This phrase concludes each section (Lev. 1:9, 13, 17) and captures the double character of sacrifice. From the human side the sacrifice is offered in obedient response to Yhwh's instructions and is consumed by fire. The corresponding divine response is the acceptance of the aroma of the sacrifice. Since this phrase is usually not associated with the purification or reparation offering, Milgrom argues that it has a positive function (the LXX has osmē euōdiás, 'scent of perfume'). However, it is also possible to interpret this in a way that is consistent with a nuance of atonement. Watts (2013:210–12) suggests 'soothing scent', since nuances of appeasement and atonement are found in texts that refer to the use of incense in checking the wrath of God (Num. 16:46).

# The grain or cereal offering (Lev. 2; 6:14-18 [Heb. 6:7-11])

Outside P the word for this sacrifice (minḥâ) can be used for a gift (Gen. 32:13) or tribute (Judg. 3:15). In Leviticus it refers to various forms of grain offering. Its location here as the only non-blood sacrifice is probably because it generally accompanies the burnt offering, although it can also be offered as an independent sacrifice. A good meal for both God and people will include meat, bread and wine. Milgrom (1991:195–6) supports the rabbinic understanding that it is the poor man's burnt offering. However, it is found in a wide range of rituals, mainly as an accompaniment to other sacrifices. It may then reinforce the association of sacrifice with a meal with the specific implication depending on context.

The prohibition of leaven (Lev. 2:11; cf. Exod. 12–13) and the requirement for 'the salt of the covenant' (Lev. 2:13; cf. Num. 18:19) highlight how aspects of ritual can echo and reinforce the controlling Exodus narrative and its theology. Non-priestly texts imply that all the grain was offered (1 Kgs 8:64), but in Leviticus 2 only a handful is offered as a representative or token portion, with the rest going to the priests. The priests alone are able to eat it because of its most holy status. It is prepared at home, offered by the priests and then eaten in a Holy Place (Lev. 6:14-18). The different forms of this sacrifice highlight the flexible nature of the form and function of any particular sacrifice.

# The well-being offering (Lev. 3; 7:11-18, 28-34)

This sacrifice is usually called the sacrifice of well-being (*zeḇaḥ šᵉlāmim*). Both terms are ancient and in non-Priestly texts they tend to appear separately. However, we do not know enough to reconstruct a history of this sacrifice, and the combination of the two may well be a comprehensive phrase for all sacrifices that result in the consumption of meat. The first term (*zeḇaḥ*) simply means 'slaughter', but the meaning of the second is uncertain (*šᵉlāmim*). It is derived from the root *šlm*, which means 'be well, be whole, be complete'. The presence of this root in the Hebrew word for peace (*šālôm*) is the reason for the translation 'peace offering', but the more general idea has led to 'well-being offering'.

The best guide to the meaning of this sacrifice is its character rather than its etymology. The distinctive feature is the provision of meat for the offeror and his family. Offering a costly sacrifice is a rare event and cause for celebration in a subsistence rural society. It is never associated with atonement and could probably be offered on its own, although in certain rituals it is combined with other sacrifices. Leviticus 7 indicates that there were several different kinds of well-being offering. The freewill offering (*nᵉḏāḇâ*) is a voluntary sacrifice without any special association. A votive offering (*neḏer*) follows the successful fulfilment of a vow (e.g. Gen. 28:20-22). A thanksgiving offering (*tôḏâ*) acknowledges the happy outcome of some venture. Although there is an element of acknowledgement of God for his benefits ('praise', Hartley 1992:41), the main emphasis is on the social and the covenantal, resulting in a strengthening of the community (Gorman 1997:32). This is conveyed by alternative translations such as 'fellowship offering' (NIV) or 'communion offering'.

# The purification or sin offering (Lev. 4:1–5:13; 6:24-30 [Heb. 6:17-23])

The significant stage of this sacrifice is the manipulation of blood, which has as its goal atonement. It is required in four different situations (Marx 1989): inadvertent transgressions on account of ignorance or error (Lev. 4), major impurities (12:6; 14:19; 15:15, 30), the consecration of priests (8:14; 9:7) and the annual festivals (Num. 28–29). The first of these has been the main evidence for the traditional translation 'sin offering', especially since the name of the sacrifice (*ḥaṭṭā't*) is the normal word for sin. Its use in consecrations and festivals could relate to sin and/or impurity. However, there is no overt implication of sin in its use in relation to serious impurities arising from, for example, childbirth (Lev. 12). Furthermore, the equivalent form of the verb can be translated 'purify' or 'cleanse' (e.g. 8:15; 14:49) when it describes the effect of blood. Since it is likely that the Priestly writing understands sin as also producing impurity, 'purification offering' recognizes the broad scope of this sacrifice, which can deal with both physical impurity (resulting in purification) and sin impurity (resulting in forgiveness and purification).

If we include the Day of Atonement there are three distinct blood rituals, depending on where in the sanctuary the blood is applied.

1  If the offender is a ruler or an ordinary person (Lev. 4:22-35), then it is sufficient for a priest to take some of the blood and put it on the horns of the altar in the courtyard of the Tabernacle, with the rest poured out at the base of the altar (v. 30). The offerors do not benefit from the food

of the animal (a female goat or male lamb), but the priest may eat parts of it (6:26 [Heb. 6:19]).

2  If the anointed priest or the congregation has offended (Lev. 4:3-21), the High Priest takes the blood into the outer room of the Tabernacle. Some of it is put on the incense altar, while the rest is sprinkled seven times before Yhwh (vv. 17-18). The heightened seriousness of the sin/ impurity is also indicated by the cost and prestige of the animal used, a bull. None of the sacrifice may be eaten, since the priests are also at fault.

3  In the unique ritual on the Day of Atonement the concern is all the sins and impurities of Israel (see further ch. 7). The High Priest brings the blood of a male goat into the innermost sanctum, the Holy of Holies, and sprinkles it upon and before the cover of the ark (Lev. 16:15).

# The reparation or guilt offering (Lev. 5:15-19; 6:1-7 [Heb. 5:20-26]; 7:1-10)

This reparation offering (*ʾāšām*) has the same root as a verb that also appears in the instructions for the purification offering (Lev. 4:13). A similar ritual is followed (7:7), implying that the two sacrifices are closely related. The meaning of the verb is disputed. The traditional translation of the verb assumes an objective nuance: 'incur guilt' (NRSV) or 'are guilty' (AV). But in some texts the sin happens before the action indicated by the verb. So others propose 'realize guilt' (NJPS; Kiuchi 1987:33–4), 'feel guilt' (Milgrom 1991:339) or 'suffer guilt's consequences' (Sklar 2005:39–41). In Hebrew the same word can indicate both the action and the consequences of that action, depending on context. So NRSV translates the normal word for sin in Leviticus 5:6 as 'penalty for sin', referring to why this sacrifice had to be offered. Since the sacrifice deals with the consequences of various kinds of fraud, it is more accurately translated 'reparation offering'. The traditional 'guilt offering' implies an overly subjective and individualistic interpretation.

The three cases cited involve inadvertent trespass: sin against a holy thing (5:15-16), sin against a prohibitive commandment (5:17-19) and a false oath leading to damage against a neighbour (6:1-7 [Heb. 5:20-26]). The distinctive feature is that financial reparation to the injured party is required, amounting to the cost plus a fifth, as well as a sacrificial ram (6:5

[Heb. 5:24]). Confession of the wrong is also mentioned in Numbers 5:7. The result, as for the purification offering, is atonement and forgiveness (5:16, 18; 6:7 [Heb. 5:26]).

# Atonement

A key term in the discussion of sacrifice is the Hebrew verb *kpr*. The variety of ways in which it is used have puzzled interpreters and frustrated translators. The traditional English translation 'atone' implies two parties reaching agreement (at-one-ment), but the idea of reconciliation is not explicitly found in Priestly texts. 'Atone' is a traditional rendering that is best understood as a technical term that does not in itself imply any specific interpretation. Atoning sacrifices are restorative or corrective, dealing with impurity and/or sin. The object of atonement can either be a Holy Place (Lev. 16:20) or people (4:26; 9:7; 12:7).

Translations often reflect a focus on the removal of sin ('expiate') or impurity ('purify', 'purge', Milgrom 1991:1079–81). Other recent proposals seek to embrace the flexibility and openness of the term, for example 'mitigate' (Watts 2013:343–6) or 'clear' (Hundley 2011:191). Past interpreters sometimes laid great weight on the meaning of the cognate verb in other languages such as Arabic ('cover') or Akkadian ('wipe'). However, the contexts in which the cognates appear are so different that this is of little help (Feder 2010).

One area of debate is whether the use of the root is similar in cultic and non-cultic contexts. The verb 'atone' uses the same letters as a noun meaning ransom (*kōper*), and atonement and ransom are related in two texts. In Exodus 30:11-16 the census money is described as a 'ransom for his life to Yhwh', and it serves to 'atone for your lives' (*lᵉkappēr ʿal-napšōṯēkem*, the phrase is also found in Lev. 17:11). Similarly, Numbers 35:31-33 asserts that there is to be no ransom for the life (*nepeš*) of a murderer, and only the murderer's blood can atone for a land polluted by shed blood. These texts also encourage an association with the idea of substitution. A ransom takes the place of the person, just as an animal dies in the place of the offeror who deserves to die because of their sin. This approach can be further developed in seeing sacrifice as the answer to God's wrath against sin. Kiuchi (2007:47, 57) even proposes the translation 'make propitiation', since the blood serves to appease God's deadly anger against the sinner. However, there is little emphasis on wrath in the cultic texts, and the commercial concept of ransom is also foreign to the world of the cult.

These two key texts probably reflect a later interpretation. This would also be the case for Leviticus 17:10-12, which seeks to explain why Israelites are prohibited from 'eating blood'. This probably refers to eating a sacrifice without the proper disposal of the blood. Because these verses associate the atoning power of the blood life, it can be claimed that atonement is primarily a positive rather than a negative concept (Gese 1981; Janowski 1982:242–7). The offeror identifies with the sacrificial animal through laying on a hand, and its blood (released by death) enables the person to come into contact with God in the Holy Place. Drawing near to God in this way enables Israel to become a holy people (Lev. 19:2). However, the emphasis of the texts is that an atoning sacrifice is a restorative ritual, and the positive dimensions are expressed elsewhere.

Milgrom (2000:1469–79) has alternatively argued that these verses refer only to the well-being offering. Killing an animal is equivalent to manslaughter (Lev. 17:3-4; cf. Gen. 9:6), thus making the life of the offeror forfeit. Benefiting from this sacrifice is only possible because the blood of the animal acts as a ransom for their life. However, the previous verses refer to burnt offerings as well (Lev. 17:8-9), and there is little evidence that killing animals was regarded as manslaughter.

# A black box theory

It is possible that the Priestly texts are open to several different interpretations of sacrifice. They are able to coexist because they all acknowledge the central role of sacrifice in achieving a range of goals. A black box model of sacrifice emphasizes our ignorance of the inner workings of the box (the process of sacrifice) but focuses attention instead on the input or stimulus (e.g. impurity) and the resulting output (purification). The mechanism of sacrifice is complex and mysterious (the black box), but the important point is that it is effective, whichever explanation or model is favoured.

It is necessary to relate Leviticus's portrait of sacrifice to modern terms and concepts for us to understand, but this is both valuable and potentially misleading. When scholars imply that sacrifice is or is not like something, they are exploring its meaning in terms of a theological concept or metaphor known from elsewhere. In order to do this they are necessarily selective.

**Figure 4** The sacrificial system

| Reason for sacrifice | Sacrifice (black box) | Result of sacrifice |
| --- | --- | --- |
| *Negative – restoration* | | |
| major impurity | purification offering | purification |
| inadvertent sin | purification offering | purification and forgiveness |
| inadvertent damage | reparation offering | purification and restitution |
| *Positive – strengthening* | | |
| praise, honour, homage | burnt offering | acceptance |
| corporate celebration | well-being offering | fellowship |
| thanksgiving | well-being offering | |
| *Transitional – change of status* | | |
| sons of Aaron | ordination offering | priestly consecration |

The danger is thinking that sacrifice is thereby 'explained' by proposing that it is 'really' about violence, forgiveness, substitutionary atonement and so on. But from the perspective of the ancients this reverses the target of the explanation. Sacrifice is the foundational reality through which other concepts can be better understood. Each interpretive concept can be helpful so long as it respects the non-reducible complexity of sacrifice. Interpretive wisdom is to be found in working with several overlapping and complementary metaphors and models, rather than one comprehensive theory.

Figure 4 above recognizes that we can distinguish three main reasons for sacrifice (Gorman 1997:7–8). The first is maintenance, the task of protecting the relationship with God from forgetfulness and presumption, while positively enhancing communication with him and an appreciation for all his gifts. The burnt offering (setting aside the atoning aspect) is an important means for deepening the relationship with God, and the well-being offering celebrates God's gracious provision in the context of the family and the covenant people. The second function is corrective or restorative. Sacrifice corrects fault in the system that will eventually become deadly. What is important is that the appropriate purification or reparation offering will deal with the specific problem (sin, impurity). A third purpose of sacrifice is transitional, as when a priest is ordained with the help of an ordination offering. The ritual relating to skin disease (Lev. 14) is also transitional, reincorporating the sufferer into the community. The ancient world never questioned the efficacy of a properly performed sacrifice. The main concern was that it be appropriate in form and consonant with tradition, though not necessarily identical. The diversity of cases described in Leviticus and elsewhere suggests that the need for innovation and flexibility was acknowledged.

# Reflections on sacrifice

A systematic rationale for the sacrifices of Leviticus remains a disputed possibility rather than an agreed assumption. The texts reflect different perspectives that suggest a system that was by no means fully worked out. An approach that emphasizes sources and historical development will tend to emphasize change and inconsistency. Yet others find sufficient coherence that they believe it possible to formulate an underlying structure and theology.

One of the difficulties is what we mean by 'explanation'. Discussions of sacrifice often seek to explain it from a modern framework of meaning. However, sacrifice in Leviticus is interwoven with numerous other aspects of life so that it is hard to fix on one feature that will illuminate all. Douglas (1999) suggests that P reflects what she calls analogical thinking, rather than the rational-instrumental quality of thinking demonstrated by Deuteronomy and more familiar to the modern world. Leviticus 1–7 represents a set of symbols and actions that inform an embodied and implicit knowledge of God, people and world that is consistent and life-giving.

Reflection on sacrifice is enriched through engagement with the narrative of Leviticus. Sacrifice is Yhwh's gracious gift to a sinful, impure and needy people. Obedient recourse to the right sacrifices enables individual and nation to renew their covenant identity and discover Yhwh's favour and blessing. The presumption of the text is that the Israelites will be willing participants in the system. The breaking of this presumption will be one of the targets of the prophetic critique of sacrifice (Isa. 1:11; Hos. 6:6).

# 4

# Priesthood
# (Leviticus 8–10; 21–22)

## Priesthood in Leviticus

Leviticus has a great deal to say about priests and priesthood. Indeed, the title in the Septuagint (*Levitikon*) indicates this, although it assumes an identification of Levites and priests that is found in traditions other than P (e.g. Deuteronomy). On this understanding it is the equivalent of the rabbinic title of the book, *torat kohanim*, the manual of the priests (Meg. 3:5; Menah. 4:3). However, the Priestly view is that Levites are not holy in the cultic sense. Although they do have special roles, they are on the same level as the other tribes in not being able to move in holy places and touch holy things.

Priests are key figures in most of the rituals, especially the laws of sacrifice (1–7), so that it makes sense for the next section of Leviticus to describe the ordination of Aaron and his sons (8–10). The extensive discussion of priests in Leviticus 21–22 is generally assigned to H, but it is consistent with the portrayal in 1–16. Priestly holiness is both ontological (a matter of lineage) and functional (active performance). Priests have to belong to the Aaronite clan and are born into a priestly family. The danger of compromising this birthright is probably why those whom a priest can marry is strictly delimited (Lev. 21:7-9). A mixed marriage, or one where there is doubt about the mother, would endanger inherent holiness. A priestly family shares in some way the holiness of the priests, since they can eat the priestly portions of the well-being offering (10:14). However, active priestly ministry begins with donning the distinctive priestly clothing, which is consecrated along with the priests (8:30). It is implicit that this ceases when a priest puts off his priestly clothing and leaves the sanctuary, since holiness and impurity are incompatible.

What was at the heart of the priestly calling, according to P? Priests in Israel did many things: they tended the sanctuary, offered sacrifices, taught, blessed, judged, advised, divined. One possible unifying theme is that the priests were mediators between God and the people. They represent Yhwh to the people and the people to Yhwh as they move between the holy and the profane. As is the case in the Ancient Near East, the main modes of mediation were sacrifice, divination and instruction (Kugler 2009:597). To this we should add blessing in the name of Yhwh (Num. 6:22-27). Both sacrifice and blessing are mentioned at the conclusion of Aaron's ordination (Lev. 9:22). The priests receive the sacrificial animals at the entrance of the Tent of Meeting (12:6; 14:11) and offer them on the main altar in the courtyard (Lev. 1:5; 2:2; 3:2). Those who brought the animals kill them, but priests deal with the blood and the burnt portions of the animal and dispose of the remains. Blessing is a vital means of communicating the life-giving presence of Yhwh to the people so that they can flourish and live in security (26). Divination is less prominent, since divine commands are usually given in speech, but a limited option is provided in the Urim and Thummim (Exod. 28:30). Instruction is also specified with a focus on cultic matters of holiness and impurity (Lev. 10:10-11).

However, mediation may be too general a term. Israel has other figures (patriarchs, prophets, kings) who are also mediators. The focus in Leviticus is that priests are consecrated so that they can minister or serve (*šrt*) in the sanctuary (Exod. 30:20; 39:1; Leithart 1999). Metaphorically Yhwh is the great king, whose temple is his palace, and so has attendants who look after it and perform the necessary housekeeping tasks. Since the Tabernacle/Temple links heaven and earth, he has both heavenly servants (e.g. the cherubim, 25:20) and earthly ones, the priests. The other Levitical clans also assist, but this is more hard service ('*ăbōdâ*) in tending to the equipment of the Tabernacle without entering into its holy space (Exod. 38:21; Num. 1:50). Although Leviticus does not use the language, 'servants of the sanctuary' summarize much of the priestly role. Their wider role in matters of impurity (Lev. 13-14) also serves the sanctuary in dealing with threats to its holiness (15:31). They were interpreters of the proper boundaries of holy space, time and status (10:11; Duke 2003:652), whose proper observance maintained the continuing presence of God that was essential for life and blessing (ch. 26). Discerning and communicating the dates of festivals was a particularly important task in ancient cultures (see ch. 6). The priests were to sound the trumpets on the first day of the seventh month (23:24) and on the Day of

Atonement in the Jubilee year (25:9). The sanctuary played an important role in the most important of these festivals (23).

In return for their service, Yhwh supplies the needs of the priests and their families. They receive the majority of the grain offering (Lev. 2:3), and the discussion of sacrifices in Leviticus 6–7 pays special attention to priestly portions. The well-being offering is the main source of meat, with the priest receiving the breast and the thigh (7:30-36). Those who needed to sacrifice a purification offering or reparation offering could not benefit from it, but the priests did (6:29 [Heb. 6:22]; 7:6). The priest also received the skin of the burnt offering (7:8).

Most priestly requisites could be shared with the family, but the purification and reparation offerings had the status of being most holy and so could only be eaten by the male priests. Perhaps the major source of income was the tithes of grain, fruit and livestock brought by the people to the sanctuary. Since these were holy to the Lord (Lev. 27:30), they belonged to the priests, who shared that state of holiness. Priestly families also benefited from those who made vow (27:1-13), the consecration of a person or property to the Lord (vv. 14-29), the dedication of first fruits (2:14-15; 23:10), and the offering of firstborn animals (27:26-27; cf. Num. 18:15-18). Interaction with the holy God could be dangerous (10:1-3), but it brought rewards that could lead to resentment and jealousy (Num. 16).

# The priests and the High Priest

The first substantial discussion of priests in Leviticus comes in the narrative of their ordination in Leviticus 8–9. This descriptive account of the inauguration of the priesthood corresponds to the prescriptive account of Exodus 28–29 (Levine 1965). It is presented as a unique founding ritual (Gorman 1990:103–39), so it is not clear how far it was also intended to describe the ritual for the ordination of future generations of priests. The ritual is what anthropologists call a rite of passage, in which a person is brought from one status to another through a liminal period of preparation. Before the ordination ritual Aaron and his sons have no special priestly status, although previous narratives have anticipated Aaron's later pre-eminent role (e.g. Exod. 16:33). At its conclusion the priests have been fully consecrated and possess the holy status that allows them to act as priests in the Holy Place. As the founder of the nation and Yhwh's special representative, Moses officiates as an interim priest, offering sacrifices and anointing the priests and the Tabernacle. Leviticus 8 describes the initial rite of separation, parts of which may be repeated during the seven days (Lev. 8:33-34). The chapter is divided into seven sections, marked by the repeated formula 'as Yhwh commanded'. The occurrence of this phrase seven times in the account of the manufacture of the priestly garments (Exod. 39) and the assembling of the Tabernacle (40) reinforces the association of person and place. The eight-day ritual concludes with a rite of incorporation, where Aaron confirms his priestly status by offering sacrifices and giving a blessing (Lev. 9). The appearance of the glory of Yhwh and the consumption of the burnt offering and the fat on the altar by divine fire seals the process and witnesses to the effectiveness of Aaron's priestly ministry (vv. 23-24). In the narrative framing of Leviticus the subject of the ordination ritual is Aaron and his sons. It is unclear how far the ordination ritual of Leviticus 8–9 was intended to be unique or repeated.

The special ordination sacrifice is derived from the word for 'filling', corresponding to the standard idiom for ordaining the priest, 'filling the hand' (Exod. 29:33; cf. Judg. 17:5, 12). The origin of this idiom is obscure, although it perhaps derives from how the hands of a priest are filled with sacrificial portions (Lev. 8:27-28) or even wages (Judg. 17:10). The blood of the ordination sacrifice is daubed on the right ear, thumb and toe (Lev. 8:23-24), probably representing the whole through the extremities. Less likely is Gorman's suggestion (1990:131–5) that the blood (representing life) gave the priests safe passage across the dangerous boundary between the holy and the common.

The nearest equivalent to the ritual is the purification of someone with scale disease. This also includes a seven-day period, ritual washing, stationing at the entrance of the Tent of Meeting and daubing blood on the extremities (Lev. 14). In both cases it is stated that the ritual is effective on the first day (priests are consecrated, 8:30; the person with scale disease purified, 14:8). But the ritual is only completed at the end of the seven days. While the language of P is binary (e.g. clean/unclean, holy/profane), the ritual indicates a more complex and staged transition. The symbolic and chronological complexity conveys the many-sided significance of what is being achieved, as well as giving the ritual an appropriate weight and significance.

There is a difference in kind between their holiness of the priests and that of the Levites and the rest of the people. There is also a difference in degree of holiness between that of the High Priest and the priests (Jenson

1992:115–48). He is called the High Priest or more literally the great priest (*hakkōhēn haggāḏôl*, 21:10). The qualitative difference between Aaron the High Priest and his sons is emphasized in three main ways. The first is their differentiated clothing. Moses clothes Aaron with seven items of priestly clothing, whereas his sons only receive three, and these are also listed later, after the ritual of the anointing oil (Exod. 28; Lev. 8:6-13). Moreover, the materials of the high priestly clothing correspond with the materials of the Tabernacle (Haran 1978:160–74), aligning the holiness of the High Priest with the holy areas in which he ministers. Anointing is a second way in which the High Priest is marked out. Moses anoints the Tabernacle and Aaron's head first (Lev. 8:10-12), indicating that Aaron has the level of holiness that enables him to access even the Holy of Holies. Only at the end of the chapter are Aaron's sons also anointed and consecrated, when Moses sprinkles some of the anointing oil and blood on the sons and their garments (v. 30). The distinction corresponds to the main areas of service. Aaron's role is primarily within the Holy Place, while the typical ministry of his sons concerns the standard sacrifices on the bronze altar in the courtyard. The literary style and structure of the texts are a third indicator of difference. Aaron and his sons are all involved in the special rituals relating to the unique ram of ordination (Lev. 8:22-28). Aaron and his sons undergo the same ritual, but Aaron is always mentioned first, and the daubing of the blood is noted first for Aaron and then for his sons.

The unique holiness of Aaron and his successors is reflected in his special priestly duties, as well as limits on his personal freedoms (see the next section). The focus of his role is within the sanctuary proper, in the Holy Place, whereas the ministry of his sons is in the courtyard. Within the Holy Place every week Aaron is to trim the lampstand (24:2-4) and renew the twelve loaves on the gold table (vv. 5-8). He offers the purification offering when he himself sins (4:3-12). The High Priest has the primary role in the weighty sanctuary rituals of the Day of Atonement. While his own status is unique, his supreme status in the priestly hierarchy enables him to represent the people on such occasions. He alone enters the most Holy Place, where he atones both for his and the people's impurities and sins (16:11-19), before laying his hands on the scapegoat and confessing the sins of Israel (vv. 20-22). This representative function is highlighted by the comment that his own sin brings guilt upon the people (4:3), as well as the close similarities between his purification offerings and that of the people (vv. 13-21).

Yhwh addresses Aaron along with Moses regarding the laws of impurity (Lev. 11:1; 13:1; 15:1). The High Priest is responsible for ensuring that the priests teach these laws and ensure that the relevant purifications are carried out. The priests, and especially the High Priests, are leaders, but the cultic focus of their calling both highlights and limits the scope of their authority. It does not include military or tribal leadership. The priests are responsible for ensuring that the cosmic order is maintained through the proper rituals and accurate teaching. If a ruler needed atonement for unintentional sins they needed priestly mediation (4:22). Priestly advice or oversight in other spheres was optional.

The breastplate of the High Priest included the Urim and the Thummim (Lev. 8:8), which enabled the will of Yhwh to be divined and important decisions made (Exod. 28:30; Num. 27:21). They may possibly have been two stones or dice that could give a yes/no/undecided response to a question, but this is speculative. It was probably intended to be a guide to important national and military decisions (1 Sam. 14:41; Ezk. 21:18-21). It was an exception to the general prohibition of the modes of divination that were common in surrounding cultures (Lev. 19:26). Milgrom (1990:508) suggests that its restriction in P to the sanctuary was to differentiate its use from the idolatrous lot casting that was prevalent in Israel's neighbouring cultures. This would be too restrictive an interpretation if Saul's practice was regarded as legitimate (1 Sam. 28:6).

# Priestly faults

The Tabernacle, with its physical boundaries, represented the dangerous intersection between the holy God and his sinful and imperfect people. The priests were responsible for crossing that boundary and accessing the grace and mercy of Yhwh on behalf of the people. Their closeness to God meant that they were held to the highest standards, and there were the most serious implications if they became impure or sinned.

Impurity of various kinds was inevitable outside the sanctuary for everyone, priests as much as laypeople. The sacrifices for Aaron and his sons during their ordination emphasized that the priests were as much in need of purification as the people. Indeed, the high cost of a bull without blemish (4:3) indicated that they were even more necessary because of their holiness. If priests become impure, this did not affect their permanent priestly status, but they had to be purified before ministering in the sanctuary.

Because their inherent holiness was tied to belonging to a priestly family, there were restrictions on whom priests could marry. These laws reflect an intriguing negotiation between the practical recognition of responsibilities and the ideal representation of holiness (Lipka 2010). Priests may not marry someone who has had illicit sexual intercourse (better than 'prostitute'), someone who had been raped or someone divorced (Lev. 21:7). One motive would be that such relations might compromise the priestly lineage, but there may well also be a moral dimension, since holiness has ethical implications. As the one closest to God and having the highest status of holiness, the High Priest was subject to greater restrictions than priests. He was to marry a virgin (v. 13), whereas priests could marry a widow (vv. 7, 14). Priestly holy status had to be maintained and initiated. Yhwh is the one who sanctifies (vv. 8, 15), indicating the need for an ongoing maintenance of holiness, not merely an once-for-all consecration (8:30). This ongoing holiness also applies to the people (20:8) but is worked out in a different way for priest and High Priest.

The most severe threat to holiness is contact with the dead and this is forbidden in general for priests. There are some exceptions for the close family of priests (Lev. 21:1-4), but none for the High Priest (v. 11). Nor can the High Priest perform any custom associated with mourning, such as dishevelling the hair or tearing clothes (10:6; 21:10). Breaking this law will lead to a priest profaning himself, which may indicate the loss of their essential holiness and require reconsecration.

Blemished priests have an ambivalent status (Lev. 21:21-23). They are holy in so far as they can eat the most holy food, but they would profane Yhwh's sanctuary if they attempted to offer sacrifices. This prohibition might be a practical consideration that a disabled person would find it more difficult to offer a sacrifice correctly. This would be similar to the age limits for service for the Levites (Num. 4). However, the danger is of profaning the sanctuary (Lev. 21:23) and a more fitting explanation may be that it is incompatible with the perfection of God, which is expressed in bodily and moral terms. The list of twelve blemishes corresponds to those of animals that cannot be offered for sacrifice (22:22-24). Perfection of form is required for potential servants of King Nebuchadnezzar (Dan. 1:3-4) and for priests in other cultures. This may be another reflection of the underlying metaphor of God as king.

The seriousness of priestly sin is highlighted from the outset. The inauguration of the priesthood is followed immediately by a paradigmatic case as is typical of biblical accounts of gracious initiatives followed by rebellion (Gen. 2-3; 12; Exod. 32-34; Acts 5:1-11). Nadab and Abihu, Aaron's sons, offer 'strange fire' before Yhwh (Lev. 10:1-2; NRSV 'unholy fire' is misleading). An example of *lex talionis* (the law of retributive retaliation, 'the punishment fits the crime') maintains Yhwh's holiness in the face of disobedience. Fire goes out from before Yhwh and consumes Nadab and Abihu so that they die. It is a dramatic reversal of the affirming fire from Yhwh that consumed the sacrifices in Leviticus 9:24. Aaron acknowledges the necessity and justice of the action by his silence (10:3).

What was the problem with Nadab and Abihu's offering? Proposals focus on one or other of the details found in this text or other cases. The parallels to Numbers 16 (incense offering, fire coming out from before Yhwh) suggest rebellion, but the differences between the accounts allow other interpretations. Were they drunk (Lev. 10:9) or otherwise offering it with impure motives? Were they well intentioned, but ignorant of the right procedure (cf. 2 Sam. 6:6-7)? Was it that only the High Priest could offer incense in the Holy Place (Exod. 30:7)? Was it because a special blend of incense was required (Exod. 30:9; 'fragrant incense')? Was it because the fire was not taken from the altar (Lev. 16:12-13)? Was it offered in the Holy of Holies rather than the Holy Place (10:2)? Was it not commanded (v. 1) because they failed to follow instructions whose details we no longer know?

Historical critics have characteristically tried to locate a later setting for this story. Did Nadab and Abihu represent the similarly named sons of the apostate Jeroboam, Nadab and Abijah (1 Kgs 14:1, 20)? Was it intended to criticize the private offering of incense that was associated with Assyrian astral worship (Milgrom 1991:628–3)? Do those concerned represent later priestly groups that were in dispute? The speculative nature of these attempts and the impossibility of agreeing on a definitive explanation have led to reflection on the ambiguity, ambivalence and openness of biblical texts (Greenstein 1989). While traditional historical criticism tended to seek the one 'correct' meaning, postmodernist and deconstructionist readings emphasize the subjectivity of interpretation. As is usually the case, there are certain foundational affirmations that the text makes (e.g. the danger of illicit ritual action) as well as an openness to creative reflection that goes beyond the text and opens up a conversation with the world of the interpreter.

At the end of the chapter Aaron successfully defends his interpretation of Moses's instructions (vv. 16-20). Watts (2013:517) sees this as a confirmation of the priestly authority to interpret and adapt ritual procedure.

# The historical setting of the portrait of priesthood in Leviticus

There are few murkier historical topics than the development of priesthood in Ancient Israel (Cody 1969; Blenkinsopp 1995; Rehm 1992). Different sources of uncertain date present a variety of perspectives making use of terms that are not clearly defined, especially 'Levite' and 'priest'. In P only the sons of Aaron are priests, whereas the Levites belong to the same tribe but help the priests. Elsewhere the whole tribe of Levi appears to be priestly (Exod. 32:25-29; Deut. 18:1; 33:8-11). Texts may also reflect the theoretical ideals of their authors as much as historical reality. Synthesizing the scattered pieces of the incomplete jigsaw requires assumptions and theories that go well beyond the evidence. All this makes it difficult to be sure about the historical setting(s) for the portrait of priesthood in Leviticus.

The normal reconstructions of the history of priesthood assign the portrait in P mainly to the post-exilic era. Wellhausen's (1885:115–45) account is typical. According to him the heads of families originally exercised the priestly role. 'Levites' were favoured, but the term indicated those who took on a priestly specialization, rather than a member of an Israelite tribe. Eventually one clan (the Aaronides) gained precedence and other Levites were demoted to second-class status. The genealogical links to Levi are later means of unifying different traditions and bringing together the ontological and functional aspects. Cross (1973:195–215) proposed an alternative reconstruction, assuming a long-standing conflict between an Aaronic priestly group located in the South and a Mosaic ('Mushite') one found in the North. Haran (1978:76–102) located the Levites in the Northern kingdom and the Aaronides in the South.

Various passages in P are frequently interpreted as indicating exilic or post-exilic attempts to legitimate certain priestly groups or traditions and ensure authorization from the Persian authorities and acceptance from those who returned from exile. However, because the narratives and laws are set at Sinai, the identity of the various factions is obscured. Furthermore, it is almost impossible to distinguish between what has been created from nothing and what is a later embellishment of an earlier historical practice or pattern. Was 'High Priest' a late post-exilic title applied anachronistically to earlier times (2 Kgs 12:10; Rooke 2000:150, 214), or was it an old term that reflected the privileged role of the chief priest before the exile (Mizrahi 2011)? Was the anointing of the chief priest (Lev. 4:3) a post-exilic practice transferred from the anointing of the king (1 Sam. 9:16; Ps 2:2), or was anointing such a common rite that its origins were far earlier (Fleming 1998)? Resolving these historical questions lies beyond the scope of this guide, since they were of marginal concern to the Priestly writing, whose focus is on how priesthood is an essential and integral part of the larger system of Israel's worship.

# Reflections on priesthood

In critical Old Testament scholarship the value of the priesthood and their role have long been compared unfavourably to the prophetic calling. Protestant scholars gave priority to the prophetic critique of Israel's worship (Isa. 1:12-15; Amos 5:21-23) over promises of its restoration (Ezk. 40-48; Zech. 14:21). In part this was a reflection of the Reformation reaction against the excesses and worldliness of late medieval Catholicism. These conflicts led to a one-sided emphasis on prophetic criticisms of Israel's worship, in line with the criticism of the priestly opponents of Jesus in the New Testament. Suspicion of priestly ritual was reinforced by the enlightenment emphasis on the individual and the power of reason. Ritual was regarded as empty, incomprehensible or coercive. The lack of ethical content in priestly ritual instructions was a particularly serious problem. Those rewriting the history of Israelite religion proposed that the charismatic prophets were the source of ethical monotheism, Israel's great contribution to the perception of God. Priestly theology was a late, post-exilic phenomenon, a tragic decay into lifeless legalism (Wellhausen 1885:422–25).

Every aspect of this negative portrayal has been undermined or overturned over the last fifty years. The prophets intended to reform, not eliminate the temple and the priesthood. The poverty and inadequacy of disembodied individualism are increasingly recognized. The efforts of Jewish scholars and anthropologists have helped rehabilitate the importance of repetition and ritual as one of the primary ways in which communities are shaped and maintained. Ritual texts may be largely descriptive, but this is a consequence of the genre, rather than a deliberate dismissal of wider ethical concerns. The Holiness Code discusses priestly ritual and ethics with no hint of any tension between them. The way in which Ezekiel can hold together the priestly and the prophetic, the ethical and the ritual, indicates that these two modes are not inherently or essentially contradictory. In the

New Testament the criticism of ritual was against its misuse, especially on ethical grounds (Mk 7:1-23), and Jesus affirmed the role of priests (1:44).

Recent criticisms of the priesthood have explored issues of hierarchy, power and privilege resulting from the holiness of the priests and so the ritual functions that are exclusively theirs (Olyan 2000:27–37). Watts (2013:107–111) proposes that the authoritative style of the book's laws serves to confirm the hierarchical authority of the High Priest and the priests, which he relates to the early Persian period. Rhyder (2019:403) argues that the elevation of the central priesthood is the purpose of the centralizing concerns of H and P. The distinctions between the holiness of priests and that of non-priests (including other Levitical families) may well reflect disputes in the later history of the priesthood (Rooke 2000).

Yet these claims are related to an implicit and indirect reading of the texts. The plain meaning of the text is that it is a revelation of Yhwh to Moses and Aaron and is an expression of divine authority. The priesthood is thus always subordinate to the primary authority and will of God. The main role of the priests is to maintain Yhwh's holiness, not seek their own ends. There are plenty of examples of the misuse of priestly power (e.g. 1 Sam. 2:12-25), but this is not necessarily inherent to the office and its portrayal in Leviticus. Furthermore, cultic authority is distinct from political authority. Models of power and conflict may also be less appropriate than models of complementarity and cooperation, at least for the final form of the text and the ideal it presents. There is indeed a cultic hierarchy of holiness in Leviticus, but in the canonical presentation this is subordinate to the programmatic statement of Exodus 19:5-6, which defines the people as a 'priestly kingdom and a holy nation'. This is consistent with various texts in Leviticus (e.g. Lev. 11:44-45) and the frequent inclusion of Israel as the addressee of the laws. The laws of priesthood can be understood to embody a model of service rather than self-serving. Leviticus sets out a vision of a people who are enabled by the priests to draw near to Yhwh and discover his presence and blessing. The rituals that the priests perform with accuracy and authority allow this to be communicated with clarity and full consent. The priesthood is a key instrument of the covenant that shapes the faith of Israel and guards it against idolatry.

# 5

# Purity and Impurity
# (Leviticus 11–15)

## Introduction

The primary concerns of Leviticus 11–15 are matters of purity (*ṭāhôr*) and impurity (*ṭāmēʾ*). These are central categories in the Priestly quest to maintain and guard holiness (ch. 2). Purity is the neutral or standard state of people and is necessary to access the sanctuary. Impurity is completely incompatible with the holy so that Israel needs to limit the spread of impurity and undertake the necessary purifications if the sanctuary is not to be defiled (Lev. 15:31). The two narratives that frame this section emphasize the importance of the topic. The story of the death of two of Aaron's sons for offering strange fire in the sanctuary (10:1) demonstrates the danger of profaning the holy and leads to a statement about the key priestly role in distinguishing purity and impurity (v. 10). The same event introduces the account of the Day of Atonement (16:1), which acknowledges the continuing and dangerous presence of sin and impurity among the people and provides a way to deal with accumulated impurity year by year (see ch. 7).

The section opens with the dietary laws that all Israel has to observe (11), before treating particular cases of impurity. In typical Priestly fashion two chapters linked by the theme of sexually related impurity (12; 15) bracket chapters on the identification and purification of those with scale disease (13–14). The challenge in understanding the purity system is the range and diversity of impurities.

1  Creatures: various animals, fish and birds (Lev. 11).
2  Sexual processes: childbirth (12), various regular and irregular bodily emissions from the sexual organs (15).
3  Scale disease of people, clothing and houses (13–14).

4  Animal carcasses (11:31-40) and human corpses (21:11; Num. 19).
5  Certain ethical and religious sins (Lev. 18–20).

Each of these categories of impurity differs from the others in significant ways. Leviticus 1–16 (P) emphasizes various forms of physical impurity, to which no blame is attached if the necessary purifications are undergone. Leviticus 17–26 (H) adds ethical and religious actions that also defile the land. These two kinds have been variously called tolerated (or permitted) and prohibited impurity (Wright 1991; 1992:729–33), ritual and moral impurity (Klawans 2006:55–6), or physical and sin impurity (Ginsbursky 2009). These classes are not entirely distinct. Someone who does not undertake the required purification for physical impurity sins becomes guilty, thereby contributing to the defilement of the sanctuary and the land (Num. 19:20). Both physical and sin impurity are inconsistent with the holiness of God and the ideal order of things (Janzen 2004:112–14).

There are two main grades or levels of physical impurity:

1  Minor physical impurity is relatively insignificant, except that entry into the sanctuary or contact with holy things is strictly forbidden. An impure person usually simply bathes and waits until evening. Examples include touching a dead, unclean animal (Lev. 11:24) or the emission of semen (15:16).
2  Major physical impurity is sometimes called communicable or contagious impurity, since it can communicate a minor impurity to other people and objects by contact or proximity (Wright 1987:179–228). Typical sources were abnormal genital discharges (Lev. 15:2-12), scale disease (13) or the first stage of childbirth (12:2). Purification from major impurity generally required a purification offering and a burnt offering, as well as waiting seven days and bathing (12:6-8; 15:13-15).

We can also distinguish two grades of sin impurity:

1  Minor sin impurity. Some sins of an individual can be forgiven and their related impurity purified. This takes place through a purification (Lev. 4) or a reparation offering (5:14 -6:7 [Heb. 5:14-26]).
2  Major sin impurity. Leviticus 18–20 lists sins that are so serious that they cannot be atoned for and can only be dealt with by death and cutting off. Sin impurity is not directly communicable to others, although those who know about it and do nothing also become liable (Lev. 20:4-5).

The dating and setting of the purity laws are as disputed as other aspects of P. There are a few indications of purity concerns in pre-exilic texts arising from sexual emissions (1 Sam. 20:26; 2 Sam. 3:29; 11:4), scale disease (2 Kgs 5; 15:5) and corpse impurity (23:13-16), but there is nothing that indicates the level of detail found in P. So most historical-critical scholars assign the detailed exposition of impurity to the exilic or Persian period. Kazen (2015) argues that various parallels with Persian purity practices indicate an assimilation of certain customs by the Priestly editors. They provide a native response to the dominant culture and serve to reinforce the authority of the priests and the importance of the rebuilt temple. As in other areas, the selectivity of the biblical accounts and our ignorance of the character and development of P make any historical reconstruction of the development of purity laws tentative.

# Explanations of impurity

Great effort has been put into explaining the concepts of purity and impurity (Klawans 2000; Nihan 2013). The discussion has been complicated by the relative absence of these concepts in modernity with the temptation to reclassify them in more congenial terms (e.g. 1 and 2 below). However, anthropologists and historians of religion have highlighted the universality of these concepts and their continuing power in certain areas, especially the realms of sex and death. For P such categories were central to the identity of a man or woman and as real (or as illusory) as the categories that we make use of in the modern world (e.g. brain, ego, feelings). Categories, concepts and experience are inseparable (Lakoff and Johnson 2003). The concern of the texts was not to explain but to provide guidance for living safely within a particular understanding of God and the world. The range of impurities makes it difficult to provide a persuasive and comprehensive account. The complexity of the discussion can be sampled by the following list of explanations. These should be evaluated by how well they make sense of the range of impurities, as well as their capacity to bridge the conceptual gulf between the conceptual world of Leviticus and that of today.

1  The hygienic explanation. Earlier scholars employed medical language to rationalize a number of the sources of impurity such as the quarantine imposed on the person with scale disease (Lev. 13). Unclean creatures are unhygienic or can lead to diseases. The pig is prohibited because

diseases such as trichinosis can come from eating undercooked pork. However, this is modern rational category imposed on a system that is primarily social and symbolic. It represents an anachronistic 'medical materialism' (Douglas 1966:32).

2  The moral explanation. A traditional Christian approach is to regard impurity as a synonym for sin, an assumption reinforced by the translation 'sin offering' for the *ḥaṭṭāʾt* sacrifice (see ch. 3). Scale disease is Miriam's punishment for rebellion (Num. 12) and purification is a common metaphor for the forgiveness of sin (Ps. 51; Heb. 1:3). The second-century BC Jewish writing, the Letter of Aristeas (142-51), suggests that animals with divided hoofs are clean and edible in order to teach us the importance of discrimination that leads to the practice of virtue. Milgrom (1991:718–36) draws the general moral lesson that the dietary laws teach respect for animal life. For Kiuchi (2007:203–13), the food laws are a reminder of the fall (Gen. 3), and water creatures without fins and scales resemble the serpent who tempted Adam and Eve. However, sin and impurity overlap but are not identical. Regarding all impurity as sinful leads to strained and unnecessary explanations of normal sexual processes such as childbirth (Lev. 12) and menstruation (15:19).

3  The demonic explanation. As discussed in Chapter 3, Milgrom draws on this approach in interpreting the purification offering. In addition to the difficulties noted there, this approach struggles to explain the full range of impurities.

4  The cultic explanation. Impurity represented the idolatrous practices of the nations, which Israel was to avoid (Lev. 18:24-30). The pig was sometimes sacrificed to the powers of the underworld (Houston 1993:161–5). Ancient Near Eastern myths and practices sometimes trace fertility and blessing to the sexual union of the gods. However, for the most part other nations sacrificed the same range of animals as Israel, and most kinds of impurity derive from common human nature.

5  The structuralist explanation. This emphasizes the importance of boundaries with the laws of impurity designed to maintain the social and cosmic order of the world. Classification and boundaries are especially prominent in Leviticus 11 (see below). Nihan (2007:317–23) argues that the major impurities of Lev. 12–15 (birth, scale disease, sexuality) represent major uncontrollable biological events that intrude into the social sphere and threaten the right ordering of Israel's

life. The corresponding purification rituals are rites of passage that re-establish the proper social and cosmic order. However, this does not address fully the theological dimension of impurity, and does not do justice to sin impurity.

6  The unchanging God explanation. Unlike humans, Yhwh is eternal and unchanging. His holy, unique character is incompatible with human ephemerality, which is highlighted by impurity. Humans are only able to extend their lives through sex and childbirth, which represent how humans (unlike Yhwh) are able to transcend their mortality. Impurity thus highlights the gulf between humans and the holy, unchanging God of Israel, who is never associated with sexuality (Wagner 2018:118). This is not a matter of morality, since sexuality is assessed positively (cf. Gen. 1). It is simply inappropriate when it is a matter of drawing near to God. As with the previous approach, it is less successful in explaining sin impurity.

7  The death explanation. This might be regarded as an extension of the previous two suggestions. The most radical and threatening change of all is death, which is the most potent source of defilement (Num. 19). All the unclean birds are birds of prey or eat blood (Lev. 11:13-19). Scale disease is similar in appearance to a corpse (Num. 12). The loss of blood in menstruation and permanent vaginal discharges (Lev. 15:19-30) defile because unchecked loss of blood brings death (cf. 12:7; 17:14). Sin impurity can be included since the sanction for major sins is death. However, blood lost through wounds does not lead to impurity, and many of the unclean creatures of Leviticus 11 do not have a clear association with death.

The inadequacy of all of these explanations has made some doubt that the different kinds of impurity reflect a unified symbolic system. Perhaps it represents an accumulation of conventional, customary and moral expressions of impurity (Lemos 2013). It is possible that ideas of impurity develop and that the various texts represent different stages. It is striking that there are no laws about corpse impurity in Leviticus 12–15. MacDonald (2012) argues that H first applies this kind of impurity to priests, and then a later author, influenced by Deuteronomy 21:1-9, created the ritual in Numbers 19 to extend the law to non-priests. Historical-critical scholars also suggest that H is responsible for applying the impurity concept to major religious and ethical sins. However, even if there are conspicuous historical developments, and different kinds of impurity derive from various sources, it may be possible to provide some kind of conceptual synthesis. There are significant overlaps between some of these explanations, especially the last three. Death is the ultimate change and crossing of boundaries and threatens the proper created order. The impurity attending birth may be a powerful symbol of our mortality and ephemerality, while a number of the impure sexual emissions reflect the crossing of boundaries in an anomalous way.

These aspects of impurity are the opposite of what the cult represents, the holy presence of Yhwh. The most significant feature of impurity is that it disqualifies a person or an animal from approaching the sanctuary. Anything touched by death, ephemerality or disorder cannot be associated with the holy, creator God. Yhwh is the source of life and blessing who cannot be associated with death. He is the one who does not change and abides through each generation. He is not a transient being who can only live on through sexual reproduction. The ordered construction of the Tabernacle (like that of creation) reflects his ordered perfection. Admittedly concepts such as order, boundary and mortality are abstract and potentially anachronistic categories. But the use of such terms is essential in bridging the gap between past and present. The following chart (Figure 5) seeks to bring the various categories together (based on Ginsbursky 2009:13):

The fundamental poles in this scheme are Yhwh (the source of life and order) and that which is not Yhwh (death, disorder, sin). Impurity marks the boundaries between these two poles, but in various degrees. The unavoidable character of impurity emphasizes that in certain respects humans do not belong to the realm of the divine. Natural bodily processes lead to minor impurity, but this is result of the created order and can be easily removed by waiting for a day and washing. More serious is major impurity, which is associated with mortality and death, and affects not just the individual

**Figure 5** The impurity system

|  | Life/Order |  | Death/Disorder |
| --- | --- | --- | --- |
| physical impurity | minor/normal | major/abnormal | – |
| sin impurity | – | certain sins | idolatry, sexual sins, murder |
| object of defilement | Individual | individual + sanctuary | individual + sanctuary + land |
| means of removal | non-sacrificial | atoning sacrifice | death and/or cutting off |

but also the sanctuary. It therefore requires sacrificial purification. Lesser (inadvert) sins also fall into this category, because they disrupt the moral order and are contrary to Yhwh's righteous character. The sacrifice that deals with the impurity deriving from sin requires the sacrificial purification of both sinner and sanctuary (Lev. 4). Most serious of all are the major sins noted in Leviticus 18 and 20 (especially murder and idolatry). The impurity associated with these endangers the land as well as the individual and the sanctuary (18:24-30). They cannot be dealt with by sacrifice but require the death and cutting off of those responsible. Such sins are inconsistent with the ongoing presence of the holy God who dwells in the midst of Israel. If unchecked, such impurity will lead to exile (v. 28). Unlike major physical impurity major sin impurity is not communicable, perhaps because those committing these sins have separated themselves from their family and people. Their sin impurity still defiles the sanctuary but is presumably dealt with in the comprehensive atonement achieved on the Day of Atonement (16:16, 21). The goal of Israel's sacrificial system is restoring the people to a state when they can continue enjoying the presence and blessing of Yhwh in their midst.

# Leviticus 11: Clean and unclean animals

The laws of Leviticus 11 describe creatures that may be eaten or are 'unclean for you' (Lev. 11:8). This probably indicates not an inherent status (they are part of the good creation, Gen. 1), but an indication of what animals are fit or not for eating or for sacrifice at Yhwh's table (Lev. 5:2; Marx 2001:368–9). Only animal carcasses defile, similar to that of human corpses. The first part of the chapter sets out two criteria for recognizing clean and unclean animals: divided hoofs and chewing the cud (Lev. 11:2-8). A similar double criterion (fins and scales) is provided for fish that may be eaten (vv. 9-12). However, a simple list of twenty unclean birds then follows (vv. 13-19). The double test returns for winged insects, which have to walk on all fours and have jointed legs (vv. 20-23). The second part of the chapter concerns instructions for what happens when a dead creature touches people or other things (vv. 24-40). An emphatic prohibition against eating swarming creatures (vv. 41-43) precedes the chapter's climax, a reference to the holiness of God and a call to Israel to be holy (vv. 43-45).

The dietary laws are a key test for the various explanations of impurity (see the previous section and Houston 1993:68–123). The structuralist approach has been particularly influential due to the innovative writing of the anthropologist Mary Douglas (1966:41–57). Her understanding of holiness as wholeness and perfection led to the suggestion that impurity indicated that which did not conform to the proper class. Leviticus 11 classifies creatures according to their mode of movement and those that did not follow these expectations were identified as unclean (e.g. insects that fly like birds but walk on fours like land animals, Lev. 11:20). However, her analysis was based on a number of errors (Milgrom 1990:177–28, 184), and she invokes the additional criterion of association with death in order to explain the list of unclean birds. Although there is a clear classificatory concern, it is more likely that the criteria were chosen to fit the creatures that were understood to be edible or inedible on other grounds. The additional rule about chewing the cud may have been added to eliminate the pig, perhaps because of its association with consumption of human waste or rites associated with the cult of the dead (Houston 1993:167–77). Nevertheless, the attention to classification reflects a passion for order that has deep roots in the theology of creation also evident in Genesis 1.

Douglas emphasized the social function of purity laws. This was extended by Milgrom (1991:722, 725) in a grand analogy between persons, animals and geography, extending out from the holy centre:

|  | *Holy* | *Israel* | *Humanity* |
|---|---|---|---|
| Persons | Priests | Israel | Mankind |
| Animals | Sacrifices | Few animals | All animals |
| Space | Sanctuary | Land | Earth |

For example, both priests and sacrificial animals are disqualified if they have blemishes (21:17, 21; 22:17-20). Milgrom also finds a dynamic movement towards holiness, since all of Israel is commanded to sanctify themselves through obedience to the commandments and so become holy (11:44-45). However, the basis for aligning the second and third divisions is unclear, as is the relation between the general holiness of Israel and the particular holiness of priests.

The call to general holiness found in Leviticus 11 (Lev. 11:44-45) is found several times in the Holiness Code (19:2; 20:7, 26). Whether this text belongs to the Holiness School or not, it is an appropriate exception to the particular holiness that is primary in Leviticus 1–16, since the dietary laws apply to all Israel. Unlike the involuntary impurities of Leviticus 12–15, the people are required to make a choice to follow these laws. Reference to the Exodus (v. 45) indicates that keeping these commandments is a means for Israel to acknowledge and affirm its covenantal distinctiveness. Separating and distinguishing clean and unclean animals reinforce the idea that Israel is distinguished from other nations, which in turn reflects the distinction between Yhwh, the God of Israel, and the gods of other nations. This remains the case even if many of these laws are shared by other nations. It is the idea of separation that is embedded in the text, rather than the uniqueness of the classification.

# Leviticus 12: Women after childbirth

Many of the purity laws concern sexuality and the reproductive system. Leviticus 12 describes the rituals for women who have just given birth, including the duration of major and minor impurity and circumcision (for a male child). The concluding purification sacrifices at the sanctuary may either be a lamb or (for the poor) two turtledoves or pigeons (the option fulfilled by Mary and Joseph for Jesus, Luke 2:24).

One unique feature in this text is that her impurity has two stages, the first major (comparable to that of menstruation, Lev. 12:2) and the second minor, when she is simply commanded not to contact anything holy (v. 4). Explanations reflect the standard approaches to impurity. Perhaps it shows a concern for the health of the mother and child during the first few weeks, since a state of impurity would protect her from various demands. The flow of blood at childbirth could be a symbol of death in the loss of a 'life liquid' (Wenham 1983). However, not all blood defiles (e.g. wounds). Mention of the 'blood of purification' (v. 4) may suggest that the discharge of blood opens up the way to the normal stage of purity. Whitekettle (1995) suggests that the discharges after childbirth are typical but dysfunctional. Because the woman is in a state that cannot lead to new life, she is classed as impure. The difficulty with this argument is that even natural intercourse defiles (v. 18; see further below).

Another distinctive feature of the text is the different timing of the major and minor impurities incurred by the mother after the birth of a male (7/33 days) and female child (14/66 days). Biological explanations include the theory that the female takes longer to form than the male (a suggestion found in Aristotle and rabbinic sources). Magonet (1996) suggests that an occasional vaginal discharge from the girl baby after birth requires a double period of purification for the mother, since two females are involved. A 'historical' explanation is given in Jubilees 3:8-14, where the times correspond to when Adam and Eve were created (at the end of the first and second week respectively), and then brought into Eden (on days 41 and 81). It may reflect some measure of the different status of a man compared to a woman, although the same sacrifices are required for both sexes. As is often the case the lack of an explicit rationale has meant that none of the large number of theories has proved persuasive.

The clear implication of the text is that the purified mother offered the sacrifices herself (Lev. 12:6), as was also the case for a woman purified from an abnormal vaginal discharge (15:29). From time to time P explicitly includes women in cultic legislation (e.g. scale disease 13:29; the Nazirite Num. 6:2). When the laws refer to a person (*nepeš* or *'āḏām*) offering sacrifice (Lev. 1:2; 2:1; 4:2; 13:2), it is likely that this applies to women and men (Gruber 1987), although in practice it is likely that those offering the voluntary sacrifices were predominantly men.

# Leviticus 13–14: Scale disease

These two chapters discuss the identification, consequences and purification of a condition traditionally known as leprosy. However, modern leprosy (Hanson's disease) was unknown in the Mediterranean world before the Hellenistic period. Furthermore, the Hebrew word (*ṣāra'aṯ*) appears to indicate some kind of colour and texture that can be applied not only to people (Lev. 13:1-46), but also to clothing (vv. 47-59) and houses (14:33-53). It is probably a general collective term for a variety of abnormal surface conditions. It was probably not an infectious or virulent disease, as the example of Naaman suggests (2 Kgs 5). The associated impurity is communicable in a ritual rather than a medical sense. It belongs to the class of major impurities where those who come into contact also become impure (with the degree of minor impurity). It is unlikely to have affected many people, so the reason for its extensive treatment is probably because of its symbolic significance.

The concern in Leviticus 13 is not treatment or hygiene, but the decisive recognition of the condition by a priest (cf. Lev. 10:10) so that the necessary precautions can be taken. An uncertain identification requires a waiting period of seven days before a further examination. Because of its status as a major communicable impurity the affected person has to live outside the camp and ensure that people recognize the condition, both physically and through verbal warning (13:45-46). The extreme impurity of the condition is probably because of its resemblance to that of a corpse, and if so this would give weight to the 'death' approach. A similar set of associations is found in God's punishment of Miriam (Num. 12), whose scale disease is explicitly compared to that of a corpse. Aaron prays: 'Let her not be like a corpse that emerges from its mother's womb with half its flesh eaten away' (v. 12). The disease has affected the flesh in a way similar to the decay following death.

Leviticus 14 sets out the complex two-stage purification, during which the healed person is announced clean no fewer than three times (Lev. 14:8, 9, 29). The ritual begins outside the camp on the first day before moving to outside his (or her) tent in the camp for seven days (v. 8). That stage of purification is complete on the seventh day, and on the eighth day the person is finally able to offer the appropriate sacrifices before Yhwh in the Tabernacle (vv. 10-32). The seriousness of the impurity requires a full set of sacrifices at the sanctuary (reparation, purification, burnt – all lambs), although a poor person only needs to offer the reparation offering (v. 21). The result of this elaborate process is that the person is fully integrated back into the community from both a social and a ritual perspective.

The unique aspects of the ritual demonstrate the freedom with which the spatial, personal, ritual and temporal variables are shaped in order to communicate a powerful and effective message (Jenson 1992:168–71). The initial sacrifices include one-bird that is slaughtered and another that is set free over running water, similar to the distinct but paired fates of the two goats on the Day of Atonement (Lev. 16). The powerful blood purification of the sacrificial system is complemented and reinforced by the elimination ritual of the living bird. On the first and seventh days the repeated washing of clothes and bathing in water are standard means of minor purification, but to this is added shaving of the head, which symbolizes a new birth or a new stage in life, similar to that of the Nazirite vow (Num. 6:18). The whole ritual can be understood as a rite of passage. The subject begins with the status of someone with the disease. The ritual on the first day leads into a seven-day liminal period when his condition is uncertain. The sacrifices on the final day complete the process and confirm his status as a member of the community who has full access to the sanctuary.

# Leviticus 15: Bodily discharges

Leviticus 15 sets out the laws of impurity for men and women who have normal and abnormal discharges from their sexual organs. The responsibility of both men and women in recognizing and dealing with impurity is conveyed by the chiastic structure of the chapter, with normal intercourse at the centre (Whitekettle 1991):

| A  | vv. 2b-15 | long term   | male discharges | abnormal                 |
|----|-----------|-------------|-----------------|--------------------------|
| B  | vv. 16-17 | transient   | male discharges | typical but dysfunctional |
| C  | v. 18     | intercourse | male/female     | normal                   |
| B' | vv. 19-24 | transient   | female discharges | typical but dysfunctional |
| A' | vv. 25-30 | long term   | female discharges | abnormal                 |

The reason why intercourse leads to impurity, even when it results in the gift of new life, has been much discussed. The loss of blood can be linked to death (Wenham 1983), but it is hard to include the impurity that arises from the emission of semen, which may lead to conception and new life. Unlikely is Whitekettle's (1991) speculation that the impurity of natural intercourse is because of the ambiguity to the man's penis, which is responsible for urine, a waste product. The impurity of intercourse may be the strongest evidence for the proposal that impurity indicates a general incompatibility with the nature of God, who is not to be associated with anything related to sexuality or mortality.

An important statement of the purpose of these laws concludes the chapter. The purity laws are to 'keep the people of Israel separate (*hizzartem*) from their uncleanness' (Lev. 15:31). The verb has the same root as Nazirite (*nāzîr*), which involves both a separation from impurity and a dedication to Yhwh (Num. 6:2). For the Nazirite this enables them to attain a holy status (v. 5), perhaps hinting at the same call to holiness here that is also found at the end of Leviticus 11 (Lev. 11:44-45). The unlimited defilement of the Tabernacle will lead to death, which can only be prevented by Israel's observance of the laws of purity and Yhwh's provision of the rituals of the Day of Atonement (16), which appropriately follow this warning.

# Reflections on purity and impurity

The gendered character of the impurity laws has become an area of intense interest. How far do the sex laws of Leviticus reflect a patriarchal social system that reflects the subordination and diminished personhood of women (Ellens 2008; Ruane 2013). However, it is no simple matter to relate a traditional patriarchal culture to the changed norms of today (Meyers 1988). Leviticus indicates that both women and men had equal access to many aspects of the cult. This can be obscured by the use of masculine forms of the pronoun, which generally refer to both men and women (Gruber 1987). On the other hand, there are clear gender distinctions, for example when it concerns priesthood or birth. The evaluation of the evidence can range from sympathetic to highly critical, often correlated with the background and beliefs of the critic.

Physical impurity is often dismissed as an unnecessary leftover from a primitive world view. Yet purity and impurity continue to be the source of important metaphors for virtue and evil (Lakoff and Johnson 1999:307–9). They emphasize the physical and embodied character of behaviour and counter any sharp polarization between the mind and the body, the mental and the material, the private and the public. The classic example is Macbeth, who echoes the perspective of Leviticus 18 and 20 that there is no atonement possible for those who commit murder:

> Will all great Neptune's ocean wash this blood
> Clean from my hand? No; this my hand will rather
> The multitudinous seas incarnadine,
> Making the green one red. (*Mac*, 2.2.58-61)

Impurity can be a powerful language for expressing sinful action, yet it is also not identical with sin. It can be able to articulate the experience of those who have been sinned against, especially through the abnormal crossing of bodily boundaries. Defilement language is often met in pastoral situations of illicit access to the body, particularly rape. Attempts to remedy the act can include extensive washing, reflecting shame and an awareness of fault that is real yet not derived from any sinful act of the violated person. In these contexts the language of impurity is an important resource in recognizing that not all that is wrong with the world is due to personal fault.

But impurity need not have anything to do with sin. Relating childbirth and menstruation to impurity is often thought demeaning to women, but it is possible to point to the positive value of some of the associated customs and rituals (Gerstenberger 1996:205–7). Menstruation is also far more common in today's world than in a traditional culture, where fertile women spent much of their time pregnant or breast-feeding. There can be value to rituals that acknowledge a departure from ordinary life and mark a reintegration into the life of the community. In the Orthodox Church, usually forty days after birth, new mothers undergo a special ritual called the Churching of Women (Wehr 2011). This evokes concepts of both thanksgiving and purification from impurity and sin. The Book of Common Prayer of the Church of England retains a service for the Churching of Women, but any trace of purification was removed. Leviticus can clarify that impurity need not imply anything inherently sinful in being a man or a woman. The universality of sin derives from the choices that each person makes, even though this is also an unavoidable aspect of the human condition (Gen. 3; Ps. 51).

# 6

# Holy Living (Leviticus 17–27)

## Introduction

As was noted previously (Chapters 1 and 2), the character and dating of this section, traditionally called the Holiness Code, have been extensively discussed. The emphasis of this chapter will be on the interpretation of its content rather than historical-critical questions. An outline indicates the two or three occurrences of the bracketing style of Leviticus.

| | | |
|---|---|---|
| 17 | | Laws of slaughter and sacrifice |
| 18 | | Laws about sex and worship (1) |
| | 19 | Laws of holy living |
| 20 | | Laws about sex and worship (2) |
| 21-22 | | Laws about priests and worship |
| 23 | | Holy time (1): The annual festivals |
| | 24 | Laws about worship and justice |
| 25 | | Holy time (2): The sabbatical year and the Jubilee |
| 26 | | Promises and warnings |
| 27 | | Laws about redemption |

Tests referring to sacrifice and priesthood were discussed in previous chapters, and the next chapter will treat holy time.

## Law, ethics and theology

Leviticus 17–27 includes a number of features characteristic of Israelite law.

1 There are two main forms of law. The first is apodictic law, which consists of an absolute commandment or prohibition such as those found in the Decalogue ('you shall not … '; Exod. 20:1-17; Deut.

5:6-21). The second is casuistic law ('if … then … '), referring to a specific case that clarifies an ambiguity or grey area and sets out the consequences. These are found especially in Leviticus 18 and 20. The first form highlights the grounding of the law in the will of Yhwh. The second is oriented more towards the human discernment of a crime and its fitting punishment.

2 When compared to other collections of law from the Ancient Near East, Israel's laws have an unusually high proportion of motive clauses (Gemser 1953). These give reasons why the laws should be obeyed. They invite the reader's wholehearted commitment and encourage reflection on the relation between the specific and the general. They might refer to Yhwh's character (his holiness, Lev. 19:2), his redemptive action (v. 36), or to general principles that go against the proper order of things (*teḇel*, perversion, 18:23). The motive clauses point to a rhetorical desire for readers to understand how ethical practice is the outworking of underlying theological and covenantal commitments.

3 Laws range from the general to the specific. 'Do not steal' (Lev. 19:11) is a universal ethical principle, while 'you shall not keep for yourself the wages of a labourer until morning' (v. 13) applies the principle to a particular case that could arise in Israel's culture at that time. Leviticus 19:18 ('You shall love your neighbour as yourself') was later understood as being at the highest level of generality that could sum up all the other socially oriented laws (Rom. 13:9; Jam. 2:8; Jenson 2010).

4 Israelite law is aimed at the protection of the family or clan or nation rather than the individual. A 'familial paradigm' informed Israelite ethics (Janzen 1994). The laws reinforce ideals of faithfulness, loyalty and generosity that were vital for the harmony and cooperation that were necessary for survival and flourishing. The gravest sanctions are reserved for those that destroy trust and create relational chaos (murder, sexual sins).

5 Interpreters have often assumed that the laws of the Pentateuch are realistic guides for legislators with a specific date and setting. The difficulty with this approach is not just that precise datings are difficult to determine, but also that the Pentateuch preserves several law codes that reflect different stages of Israel's life (e.g. Exod. 20–23; Deut. 12–26). As was argued for cultic law (see ch. 1), while many of the laws in Leviticus 17–27 were based on real situations, it is likely that this was not the only or even primary concern in their final editing and

inclusion in the Pentateuch. At that point many of the laws referred to a context that no longer pertained. Their purpose was exemplary and instructive, rather than absolute and unchangeable. Those who studied them would develop skill in seeing how ethical and theological principles could be applied to specific cases, even if they were exiles living outside the land. One vivid metaphor for this interpretive movement is that of climbing up and down the ladder of abstraction (Webb 2001:53).

# Leviticus 18 and 20: Forbidden sexual relations

Leviticus 18 and 20 are a matched pair, bracketing the rich theological and ethical teaching of Leviticus 19. Leviticus 18 begins with an exhortation to obedience (Lev. 18:1-5), followed by a series of absolute apodictic commandments ('you shall not', vv. 6-23). It concludes with a warning about the consequences of disobedience, exile (v. 28) and being cut off from the people (v. 29). Leviticus 20 takes the form of casuistic law ('if … then') and supplies for each case the punishment for the crime. Thus the apodictic 'do not commit adultery' (Exod. 20:14; Deut. 5:18) is found in Leviticus 18:20, though with a characteristic emphasis on sin impurity: 'You shall not have sexual relations with your kinsman's wife, and defile yourself with her.' This is then complemented in Leviticus 20 by a casuistic formulation that specifies the scope and the punishment: 'If a man commits adultery with the wife of his neighbor, both the adulterer and the adulteress shall be put to death' (Lev. 20:10).

The majority of laws concern forbidden categories of incest (18:6-18; 20:9-21), to which are added other sexual transgressions (18:19-20, 22-23; 20:13, 15-16, 18), sacrificing to Moloch (18:21; 20:2-5), and illicit divination (20:6). Burnside (2003:349–55) suggests that the somewhat different sequence of laws in Leviticus 20 is based on the Decalogue sequence of idolatry, honouring parents and adultery (Exod. 20:3, 12, 14). The law works out in more detail how Israel is to behave in the areas generally indicated by the Ten Commandments.

The most notorious texts in these two chapters are those condemning homosexuality (Lev. 18:22; 20:13). Until recently these were interpreted as an absolute condemnation of any kind of homosexual activity. This understanding has been challenged on a number of grounds. One approach is to dismiss them as culturally relative, comparable to other laws regarded as anachronistic or limited (e.g. the food laws prohibiting the eating of pork or shellfish, 11:7-12). However, these verses are found alongside weighty laws that would be regarded as reflecting universal ethical standards. In Lev. 18:19-23 the order is menstruation, adultery, sacrifice to Molech, homosexuality and bestiality. In Lev. 20:10-16 it is adultery, incest with the father's wife/daughter-in-law, homosexuality, sexual relations with a wife and her mother, bestiality. Leviticus 20 emphasizes the seriousness of these offences by explicitly requiring the death penalty for all those taking part.

A more nuanced approach is to restrict the scope of the commandment, since laws generally assume a certain set of conditions for their validity that may need to be clarified by further reflection. For example, 'Do not murder' (Exod. 20:13) does not apply in war or to judicial execution. Milgrom (2004:196) thus proposes: 'First, it is addressed only to Israel, not to other nations. Second, compliance with this law is a condition for residing in the Holy Land, but is irrelevant outside it' (see the closing exhortation, 18: 24-30). Third, it is limited to men; lesbianism is not prohibited. Thus it is incorrect to apply this prohibition on a universal scale. However, a restriction to Israel does not apply to the other laws in its context, and it might be argued that Israel was intended to be a model of ethical behaviour, rather than the exception. From a canonical point of view the laws are given at Sinai, outside the land, and the natural expectation is that they would govern Israel's behaviour both in and outside the land. The silence about lesbianism might reflect the selectivity of this law. When the issue is discussed in later texts it is condemned (e.g. Rom. 1:26). Nor are these laws narrowly about procreation (adultery can be equally fruitful). Milgrom (2000:1569) also suggests that the law extends the incest prohibitions to males with liaisons outside the forbidden degrees allowable. Again the immediate context of the law makes this unlikely. Yet another approach is through a close examination of the rather obscure wording of the law, which is more literally 'with a male you shall not lie (as) the lyings of a woman'. Some find in the final phrase a reference to anal intercourse (Olyan 1994) or to the prohibited degrees of incest (Walsh 2001), but the plural 'lyings' is more open to the traditional interpretation that it refers to any kind of sexual intercourse (Feinstein 2014:174–6).

Both chapters express a strong concern for Israel to separate itself from the nations. Their obedience to these laws gave them an ethical distinctiveness. They are not to imitate the immoral behaviour of the Egyptians and the

Canaanites, Israel's enemies in the past and the future (18:3, 24-25; 20:23). Some regard this assessment of the morals of the surrounding nations as inaccurate and fictional. It reflects the human tendency to idealize one's own nation and devalue others. Milgrom (2001:1519) detects an allusion to the Noah story, since Egypt and Canaan are sons of Ham (Gen. 10:6), who 'saw the nakedness of his father' (9:22). While Israel's behaviour often echoed that of its neighbours (Judg. 19), the intention of these laws is to sharpen the ethical boundaries that defined Israel's identity. The hyperbolic rhetoric is intended to clarify how Israel should behave, rather than imply that other nations are a 'hellish cauldron of depravity' (Gerstenberger 1996:257).

Several reasons for the laws are given. The concluding summary in Leviticus18:24-30 labels all of the prohibited practices as defiling and abominations, leading to being cut off from the people (shorthand for a divine rather than a human punishment). Leviticus 20:22-26 provides a complementary positive vision of life in the land. Because Yhwh has separated Israel from the peoples (Lev. 20:24) they in turn are to separate the clean and the unclean, resulting in holiness (v. 26). Specific laws are reinforced by a variety of terms. Adultery and bestiality defile (18:20, 23), homosexuality is an abomination (v. 22), while bestiality (v. 23) and incest with a daughter-in-law (20:12) are perversion. There is a special condemnation for the sacrifice of children to Molech, who is probably an underworld deity associated with the dead (Milgrom 2000:1555–8). This practice profanes the name of Yhwh (18:21), probably because both idolatry and a deliberate recourse to the realm of the dead are contrary to his holiness. The metaphor of idolatry as prostitution (20:5; cf. 17:7) further deepens the condemnation and may explain why the subject is treated along with sexual transgressions (contrast Deut. 18:10-12).

The laws address the sexual temptations that would exist in a group of men and women in constant close contact. Illicit sexual relationships would lead to destructive jealousy, hatred and violence. In a rural setting such relational disorder would undermine the sustained and united effort that was required to maintain life in a marginal subsistence economy (Bigger 1979). Such laws would also protect a woman from sexual exploitation and affirm her dignity based on a unique role in the family. The high standards represented by the laws are consistent with those found in the wisdom literature (e.g. Prov. 5) and the prophets (e.g. Amos 2:7). It is the men who are primarily addressed, but the laws apply equally to both men and women (as in the explicit condemnation of bestiality, Lev. 20:15-16). Men and women share joint responsibility for obeying the laws and suffer the sanctions of disobedience equally. These laws thus reflect a theology of gender complementarity that is affirmed in the Priestly creation narratives (Gen. 1:27; 2:23-24). The commitment involved in marriage provides a powerful metaphor for the exclusive covenantal relationship, reflected in the condemnation of turning to Molech or mediums as prostitution (Lev. 20:5-6). Israel's obedience to these laws will determine whether it lives (18:5) or is vomited out of the land like its previous inhabitants (v. 28).

# Leviticus 19: The laws of holy living

Leviticus 19 is probably the best known in the book, mainly because of its call to holiness and the climactic command to love the neighbour (Lev. 19:18, 34). Indeed, some have suggested that this chapter is the structural centre of Leviticus (Douglas 1999:218–31; Milgrom 2000:1364–7). The laws of Leviticus 19 consist of a wide variety of commandments, like a montage of distinct but occasionally related photographs (Willis 2009:165). There is little discernible thematic flow or structure, but key topics are right worship (e.g. Sabbath v. 3; sacrifice, vv. 5-8; divination, vv. 26, 31), harmonious interpersonal relationships (e.g. stealing, v. 11; oaths, v. 12; love, vv. 18, 34) and just dealing (e.g. partiality, v. 15; honest weights, vv. 35-36; oppression of strangers, vv. 33-34). Later Christian tradition sought to distinguish cultic, moral and civil commandments, but these are inextricably intertwined in this chapter in a way that undermines any simple divide between the religious and the mundane, the private and the public. For example, the prohibition of mixing animals, seeds and clothing materials (v. 19) is probably a deliberate contrast to the presence of mixtures in the sphere of the holy (Jenson 1992: 85–7; Milgrom 2000:1660–1). The clothing of Israelites is symbolically integrated (by way of contrast) with the mixture of linen and wool that priests wear (Exod. 28:39) and that is found in the sanctuary (25:4).

A key feature of the chapter is the multiple repetitions of what is called the self-declaration formula: 'I am Yhwh' (nine times) or the longer form 'I am Yhwh your God' (seven times). The opening statement of 'You shall be holy for holy am I, Yhwh your God' (Lev. 19:2) informs all the subsequent repetitions of the formula. The concept of holiness also underlies the prohibitions of profaning what is holy to Yhwh (v. 8), profaning the name of Yhwh (v. 12; cf. 'holy name' in 20:3; 22:32) and the instructions about the Sabbath (19:3, 30). The call of holiness thus summons Israel to adopt a distinctive approach to the whole of life that is consistent with the holiness of their God.

The appropriate response is fear of Yhwh (Lev. 19:14, 32), which reflects a recognition of his sovereignty and leads to obedience. This fear is also a practical knowledge that obedience to the law (in all its forms) is rewarded or punished appropriately (vv. 8, 17). Its personal quality encourages attention to the spirit as well as the letter of the law. This is evident in the inclusion of commands that are not specifically crimes but remain moral failures (e.g. reviling the deaf, v. 14). The motivation to obey is enhanced by recall of God's saving acts, emphasized by the concluding double reference to the Exodus (vv. 34, 36). Israel is reminded of the particular historical and covenantal action of Yhwh that is to guide their attitude to the weak (the resident alien, v. 34) and inspire wholehearted commitment to the whole law (v. 37). The mutual character of the covenant is indicated by the recurrent complementary formula: 'I am Yhwh your God.'

The combination of self-declaration formula and law is also found in the Decalogue (Exod. 20:1-17; Deut. 5:1-20), which is echoed in a number of the laws of Leviticus 19. The clearer parallels concern idols (Lev. 19:4), taking Yhwh's name in vain (v. 12), the Sabbath (vv. 3, 30), honouring parents (v. 3), stealing (vv. 11, 13) and bearing false witness (v. 11). More indirect parallels refer to murder (v. 16), adultery (v. 29) and coveting (vv. 17-18). Historical critics differ in their estimate of the explicit influence of the Decalogue, largely depending on their dating of the texts. If the editors did not know of it, then they would be drawing on principles common to the Ancient Near East (e.g. 'do not steal') or to Israel's general ethical and religious traditions. However, its influence is suggested by the number of allusions or quotations throughout the chapter. The beginning of the chapter includes a cluster of commandments (vv. 3-4), while the conclusion echoes the opening self-declaration of the Decalogue (v. 36; Exod. 20:2). Whichever the historical relationship, Leviticus 19 reflects the characteristic dual character of the Decalogue and the law more generally. Covenantal law regulates both the vertical relationship between Yhwh and Israel, and the horizontal relations between members of the covenant community, as well as others.

The importance of Leviticus 19:18 ('You shall love your neighbour as yourself') is emphasized by its appearance at the conclusion and climax of a miniseries of laws regarding interpersonal relationships (vv. 12-18). These verses draw upon a range of Hebrew words for the other: associate (ʿāmît, vv. 11, 15, 16), neighbour (rēaʿ, vv. 13, 16, 18), people (ʿam, vv. 16, 18) and brother or kin (ʾāḥ, v. 17). While these terms indicate Israelite neighbours, the commandment appears again in verse 34 applied to the non-Israelite sojourner (*gēr*), suggesting that its scope is in principle universal. Its emphatic and repeated appearance in the chapter suggests that it was regarded as a summary of the law. Rabbi Akiba (c. 50–135 CE) described it as 'the great principle in the Torah', and Jesus called it the second greatest commandment (Mt. 22:39; Mk 12:31). Jesus also outlines the practical implications in what is often called the golden rule: 'Do to others as you would have them do to you' (Lk 6:31; cf. Mt. 7:12). The negative form of the golden rule is found in the mouth of great Jewish sage, Hillel the elder: 'What is hateful to you do not do to others; this is the whole Torah; the rest is the explanation; go and learn' (b. Shab 31a; cf. Tob. 4:15; Sir. 31:15).

# Leviticus 24

This chapter follows on from the account of festivals in Leviticus 23 in that the first part treats the daily and weekly rituals in the Tabernacle. However, the second half of the chapter illustrates the overlap of cultic and ethical concerns under the general concern for maintaining holiness in everyday life (Hieke 2014:938). The behaviour of the Israelites in their words and their actions should be consistent with the ongoing holy presence of Yhwh in their midst. It is significant that the first part of the chapter highlights the role of the Israelites in the regular rituals that take place in the Holy Place of the Tabernacle. They are explicitly commanded to provide the olive oil for lighting (Lev. 24:2), and Moses represents the people in providing the loaves for the table (v. 8).

The first paragraph (Lev. 24:1-4) instructs the Israelites to supply the oil required for regular burning of the seven lamps on the lampstand (*mᵉnōrāh*, Exod. 25:31-37). The second paragraph (vv. 5-9) requires Moses, representing the people (v. 8) to provide the twelve loaves for the table of the 'bread of the presence' (Exod. 25:30). This section makes it explicit that this ritual (and others) contributes to maintaining the ongoing covenant with Yhwh. The loaves are placed in two piles (rather than two rows) of six and replaced every Sabbath. Underlying these instructions (as well as that of the incense altar, Exod. 30:1-10) is the metaphor of the Tabernacle as Yhwh's house or temple. Light, food and a pleasing aroma were standard provisions in a great house. Although Gerstenberger (1996:360) suggests that 'the feeding of the deity is not taken seriously', Gane (2004:423) emphasizes the theological tightrope that the cult walked. The symbolism acknowledges on the one hand the real presence of Yhwh, while on the other emphasizes that he did not consume food like ordinary humans. Hence the bread is never regarded as consumed by Yhwh, but given to the priests once the week ends. It is likely that only the frankincense was burned as the offering by fire at the weekly handover.

The second part of the chapter (Lev. 24:10-23) begins with a narrative about someone who combines violence with invoking the divine name, Yhwh, in a curse. This probably refers to slanderous speech against Yhwh, similar to the cursing of father or mother (Exod. 21:17; Lev. 20:9), rather than using the name to curse his opponent. The case is brought to Moses since the man is of mixed race (an Israelite mother and an Egyptian father), and Yhwh confirms that it is the duty of the congregation to stone a blasphemer to death, whether sojourner or native Israelite. The witnesses lay both hands on the offender, similar to the way the High Priest lays his hands on the scapegoat (16:21). Milgrom (2000:2113-14) suggests that this is a way of transferring sin impurity to the guilty person. However, it is more likely to be a formal identification of the one responsible. It emphasizes that those who have heard the blasphemy repudiate it and acknowledge that such language must lead to death.

The specific narrative then becomes the occasion for a wider treatment of related laws in a carefully constructed chiasm (Lev. 24:17-22). These laws apply to both resident alien and citizen (vv. 16, 22) and apply to the taking of both human life (vv. 17, 21b) and animal life (vv. 18, 21). At the heart of the symmetric pattern is the *lex talionis*, 'Anyone who maims another shall suffer the same injury in return' (v. 19). The fundamental principle of retributive justice in Israel and the Ancient Near East is that the punishment must fit the crime. However, this is not necessarily a rigid equivalence. The reference to 'life for life' may indicate a monetary compensation (Exod. 21:33-34), as much as the replacement of the dead animal with a live one. The same is likely to be true for a case of personal injury. The difficulty of weighing Shylock's pound of flesh in *The Merchant of Venice* (*MV* 4.1) is just one practical reason why a flexible principle of commensurate restitution is likely (Kim 2006). Thus, a slave who has lost his eye goes free as compensation (Exod. 21:26). This is an exception to the law in Israel, which does not take note of the class of the person, whereas in the Ancient Near East it can depend on the status of the person. However, there is a conscious contrast between these cases and that of murder, for which there is no compensation and so requires the death penalty. No vicarious talion is allowed (e.g. a child is put to death for a child), as it is in other ancient law codes. The talionic principle is intended to restrict spiralling violence and vengeance. It is at most eye for an eye and implies that the wisdom of those responsible for resolving disputes and interpreting the law should prevail over the vehemence of the aggrieved.

# Leviticus 26: Promises and warnings

In the Ancient Near East law codes and treaties often ended with a section of blessings and a longer list of curses, highlighting the consequences of obedience and disobedience. They are attributed to a variety of gods and goddesses according to their specialist spheres of authority, but in Israel it is Yhwh alone who is responsible for the whole of life. Obedience or not to his commandments determined whether the land would be fertile or infertile, and whether the nation knew victory or defeat against its enemies. The vocabulary of blessing and curse is not used (contrast Deut. 28), so these are more accurately promises and threats of divine action for good and for ill, similar to those found in the prophets. The reason for the disproportionate number of curses is no doubt the common human tendency to pay attention to threats more than promises. The Jewish medieval exegete Nachmanides noted that 'the blessings are stated as generalizations whereas the curses are stated in detail in order to frighten the hearers' (cited in Milgrom 2001:2287).

The series of promises (Lev. 26:1-13) and threats (vv. 14-33) are carefully structured. In the blessings 'I shall give' comes three times (vv. 4, 6, 11), and the climax is the promise of Yhwh's covenantal presence in the midst of his people (vv. 11-12). The blessings set out parallel situations, whereas the five sets of curses are cumulative in the form of a narrative sequence 'if … then …' (vv. 14-17, 18-20, 21-22, 23-26, 27-33). Each specific set of curses is preceded by variations on 'I will continue to punish you sevenfold for your sins.' The purpose of the chastisements is for Israel to reverse its attitude and become obedient. The climactic curse fifth concludes by reversing the promise of Yhwh's protection of the land. Another nation will settle in the land instead of Israel, which will be scattered among the nations (vv. 32-33). The Sabbath theme that appeared at the beginning of the chapter (v. 2) and which underlies Leviticus 25 is now applied to the exile. The expulsion of the people will allow the land to enjoy its Sabbaths (i.e. sabbatical years) as a fitting recompense for the sabbatical years that Israel did not keep (vv. 34-35).

Covenant (*bᵉrît*) comes six times in the chapter, referring both to the covenant with the patriarchs (Lev. 26:42) and with the Exodus generation (v. 45). Two different kinds of covenant are often distinguished: those that are unconditional and unbreakable (e.g. Abrahamic, Davidic) and those that are conditional (Sinai). This is oversimplistic, since all covenants have expectations and demands, if not conditions (Mason 2008). In Leviticus 26 the Abrahamic and the Sinaitic covenants are regarded as one and the same, albeit mediated in different ways. Israel's enjoyment of blessing flows from obedience to the statutes and commandments given at Sinai (v. 3). On the other hand, disobedience does not utterly break the covenant (v. 44). The Israelites may suffer the curses of that covenant (v. 25), but this retains a future hope of reversal when the people turn back to Yhwh. Whether this turning depends on Yhwh or Israel's action is left open by the syntax of v. 40. While many translations render the verse with a conditional ('But if they confess their iniquity …'), the Hebrew uses the standard narrative form of the verb ('and they shall confess their iniquity … '). The result is a change of fortune as Yhwh actively remembers the covenant (vv. 42, 45). The final reference to the Exodus (v. 45) once again affirms the basis for future hope in the past revelation of Yhwh's grace and power.

The dating of this chapter reflects the general diversity of opinions about the composition of the Pentateuch. The majority consensus is that the chapter in its present form is Persian and reflects the influence of various exilic and post-exilic texts (especially Deuteronomy, Jeremiah and Ezekiel). It integrates a Deuteronomic conception of covenant with a Priestly one (Nihan 2007:542). On the other hand, Milgrom (2001:2348–2) argues that the majority of the chapter is pre-exilic. Ezekiel is dependent on H rather than the reverse, and the chapter lacks terms that would be expected in an exilic text, such as the language of repentance. Exile need not refer to the Babylonian captivity, since it was a standard punishment in curse collections in the Ancient Near East. Or it could refer to the deportation of Northern Israel (721 BCE). Whatever the dating, from a canonical perspective this rhetorically charged collection of promises and threats is a powerful incentive for all future generations to obey the commandments. Only in this way will they enjoy the peace and fullness of life that is Yhwh's primary desire for his people through the gift of his covenantal presence in their midst (Lev. 26:11-12).

# Reflections on holy living

Leviticus 18–20 includes the most praised and the most criticized verses in Leviticus, the call to love one's neighbour (Lev. 19:18) and the condemnation of homosexuality (18:22; 20:13). These are often regarded as irreconcilable, but before concluding this it is necessary to explore what the texts might have meant in their context. It is tempting to read into these texts what they would mean within a contemporary framework of assumptions and values.

Thus, the love commandment requires a consideration of the very different understanding of personhood and identity that belongs to a postmodern rather than a traditional culture. What it might mean to love the neighbour 'as yourself' depends on how the self is understood. It could be 'you shall love your neighbour just as you love yourself'. However, this may draw on an anachronistic romantic or egotistic theory of the self. Milgrom (2000:1655) avoids an overly interior meaning by paraphrasing 'Love (the good) for your fellow as you (love the good for) yourself'. A more social approach is to understand 'like yourself' as defining the status of the neighbour rather than the quality of the love. The neighbour is 'like yourself' in also being an Israelite (v. 18) or a fellow human being (v. 34).

'Love' is another complex concept that is hard to disentangle from modern theories of the person (Levenson 2016). The modern psychological turn towards the inner self interprets love as a feeling or emotion that is a spontaneous and bodily reaction (Dixon 2003). But in the Hebrew Bible the heart (v. 17) is better understood as the centre of the thinking and knowing person, the integrative faculty that determines attitudes and actions. It can be commanded because this kind of love is the logical outworking of Israel's faith in a covenantal and creator God, who wills good for all.

The ongoing scholarly and popular discussion of the verses condemning homosexuality similarly highlights the influence of the interpreter's prior assumptions and their hermeneutical approach. Those who do not accept the text as authoritative might accept the traditional interpretation (a comprehensive condemnation of homosexual activity) but disagree with it. Jews and Christians who acknowledge its authority are under more pressure to reconsider its interpretation in the light of a changing cultural context. The debate is complex because a theology of sex, gender and marriage requires an integrated approach to all the texts deemed canonical, as well as later insights and developments (e.g. Webb 2001; Davidson 2007; Brownson 2013). A common move is to set some texts against others. Thus,

Brueggemann (1997:196) argues that the justice trajectory (prominent in Deuteronomy) should defeat the purity trajectory (dominant in Leviticus). But Leviticus is passionate about justice as well. Setting one biblical tradition over another may be a premature resolution to the challenge that biblical theology faces in sustaining a dialogue between all the relevant texts, in conversation with the questions and insights of the present age.

# 7

# Holy Time
# (Leviticus 16; 23; 25)

## The Calendar

The attention given to holy time and festivals in Leviticus 23 and 25, as well as the pivotal role of the Day of Atonement in Leviticus 16, deserves a separate treatment. The magnificent opening to the Priestly writing in Genesis 1 already reflects the importance of the calendar and time. The creation story concludes with the seventh day, which God sanctifies. From a literary and theological point of view holy time takes precedence over holy space (Heschel 1951:191). On the fourth day the sun and the moon are created 'for signs and for seasons and for days and years'. The word translated 'seasons' is the same as that found in Leviticus 23:2, referring to the 'appointed festivals of the Lord' (*môʿ ᵃdê yhwh*). The 'holy convocations' (*miqrā ʾê qōḏeš*) occur throughout the year. They are holy because, in contrast to ordinary time, they belong to Yhwh in a special way and are to be observed in a distinctive manner.

The theology underlying the calendar is based on the characteristic biblical affirmation that God is both creator and saviour. In accord with Genesis 1 the festivals are linked to the universal rhythm of the seasons, and the calendar is governed by the sun and the moon. According to Exodus, the year begins in the spring since this is when Israel began its independent existence as a nation. The killing of the firstborn of the Egyptians in the tenth plague, and the sparing of the Israelites through the killing of the Passover lamb, was such a key event that it became the first month (12:2). From a historical point of view the killing of a lamb may go back to some kind of spring sacrificial ritual, but it is now fully associated with the event that founded the nation. There may also have been a New Year festival in the autumn, but again this has been subordinated to the Exodus account.

How are the days and months of the year reckoned and related to these holy times, especially in a culture without clocks or good communication? The easiest system is to count the months according to the lunar cycle, and indeed the word for new moon is also the word for month. There is evidence that the new moon, the first appearance of the crescent, was regularly celebrated (1 Sam. 20:5; 2 Kgs 4:23). However, lunar months vary between twenty-nine and thirty days, and it is the sun, not the moon, which controls the agricultural seasons. A lunar year of twelve months and 354 days will soon get out of synch with the solar year (365.25 days). One possible solution is to duplicate Adar, the first month, as indicated in the Mishnah (Meg. 1:4), but the Priestly tradition gives us little indication about its own resolution of the tension.

The first and most important period of time noted in Leviticus 23 is in fact the Sabbath (*šabbāt*). The Sabbath we know now is the conclusion of a seven-day week, independent of any natural cycle. Many argue that it was originally the full moon (or the day of its celebration), since this is the meaning of the related Akkadian *šabattu* or *šapattu*. The exile is the usual customary point at which to assign the change to a regularly repeated cycle. However, the evidence for the Sabbath being related to the full moon is disputed (Hasel 1988). Other theories of the Sabbath's origin include the suggestion that it was a regular market day, an earlier Kenite practice, or inspired by a seventh day festival in neighbouring ancient Near Eastern cultures. However, all these are speculative. Exodus 16 relates that Israel's first awareness of the Sabbath came in the story of the manna, and the traditional view is that it was an original and innovative Israelite institution (Levine 1989:261). The discussion in part reflects different assumptions about the development of Israelite religion and the historicity of the relevant texts. Did the exilic editors initiate revolutionary new practices, or did they emphasize and expand certain features of pre-exilic practice?

# The structure of the festival year

Leviticus 23 classifies the seven festivals of the year (along with the Sabbath) in several different ways (Figure 6).

The Sabbath is included among the 'holy occasions' (*miqrā'ê qōdeš*). Since a holy day is to be wholly dedicated to Yhwh, work is strictly prohibited. Although *miqrā'* is often translated 'assembly' or 'convocation', it is a

**Figure 6** The festival calendar

| Festival | Day | Reference | Holy occasion | Do no work | Complete rest |
|---|---|---|---|---|---|
| Sabbath | | 23.3 | 23.3 | 23.3 | 23.3 |
| 1. Passover<br>I.14 | | 23.5 | | | |
| 2. Unleavened Bread | | | | | |
| I.15 | 1 | 23.6-7 | 23.7 | 23.7 | |
| I.16-21 | 2–6 | 23.8 | 23.8 | 23.8 | |
| I.22 | 7 | 23.8 | | | |
| 3. Waving of the sheaf | | 23.9-14 | | | |
| 4. Weeks<br>III.x | | 23.15-21 | 23.21 | 23.21 | |
| 5. Trumpets<br>VII.1 | | 23.23-25 | 23.24 | 23.25 | 23.24 |
| 6. Day of Atonement<br>VII.10 | | 23.26-32 | 23.27 | 23.28, 30, 31; 16.29 | 23.32<br>16.31 |
| 7. Booths | | | | | |
| VII.15 | 1 | 23.33-35 | 23.35 | 23.35 | 23.39 |
| VII 16-21 | 2–7 | 23.36-43 | 23.36 | 23.36 | 23.39 |
| VII 22 | 8 | 23.36, 39 | | | |

quality of time rather than place and does not always require assembling at the sanctuary (Milgrom 2000:1957–8). The middle days of the two great festivals (Unleavened Bread days 2-6; Booths days 2-7) are not holy in this sense, so work is allowed. Three holy convocations (Trumpets, Booths days 1 and 8) are described as a day of 'complete rest' (*šabbāṯôn*, Lev. 23:24, 39), a word closely related to the Hebrew word for Sabbath (*šabbāṯ*). The special character of the Sabbath and the Day of Atonement are indicated by being called a 'Sabbath of complete rest' (*šabbaṯ šabbāṯôn*, 16:31; 23:3, 32). It is likely that these distinctions reflect different levels of obligations on the people. The most severe restrictions were observed on the Day of Atonement, when no work could be carried out for the entire day (23:28) and the people were to 'deny themselves' (16:29, 31; 23:27, 29, 32). The verb often has the meaning of oppress or humiliate, and in Isaiah 58:3 it is parallel to fasting. The Mishnah (Yoma 8:1) states that on this day 'eating, drinking, anointing, putting on sandals, and marital intercourse are forbidden'.

The reference to the months is by number rather than name and so highlights the two most important months, the first and the seventh. Both these months include a multi-day festival, but in line with the Priestly sabbatical principle, the seventh month is the climax of the year. It is the only month with three festivals, two of which are not found in earlier lists (Trumpets, Day of Atonement). From elsewhere it is evident that the new moon was a significant event (Amos 8:5), but only the first day of the seventh month is marked by the special festival of Trumpets and identified as a holy occasion (Lev. 23:24). The Day of Atonement on the tenth day is unique in not being a celebration, but a day of self-denial (vv. 27-32). The purification of the sanctuary and the people on this day sets up the uninhibited rejoicing throughout the multi-day festival of Booths. The two extended festivals in the first and seventh months demonstrate a chiastic symmetry: Passover (1 day) and Unleavened Bread (7 days); Booths (7 days) and an eighth day solemn assembly. The importance of the festival of Weeks is downgraded, since it is not called a pilgrimage feast (*hag*), as in other listings (Exod. 23:16; Deut. 16:16). This may reflect a shift from an earlier threefold division of the festival year into a dual pattern. This may be a response to the similar Babylonian pattern (Nihan 2007:508–9), but with a polemical note. What was a nationalistic New Year Autumn Festival in Babylon becomes in Israel the seventh month and is closely tied to Israel's story of redemption and the revelation of the sacrificial system at Sinai.

The major festivals were linked to the agricultural year. The two multi-day festivals correspond to the barley harvest in the spring and the final ingathering of fruits in the autumn. The Waving of the Sheaf (Lev. 23:9-11) refers to the sheaf of barley that is harvested first. Fifty days later (vv. 15-16) the end of the wheat harvest is celebrated (the Greek for fifty led to it being called Pentecost). Yhwh is the creator God who has provided the fruitful land and blesses the land so that the people can live in it (26:4-5). At the same time he is Israel's saviour, and this becomes a key theme in the two great festivals. Passover and Unleavened Bread evoke the mighty acts that Yhwh used to bring Israel out of Egypt (Exod. 12). The killing and eating of the Passover lamb recalls the blood that saved the Israelites from the angel of death (Exod. 12:1-32). The eating of Unleavened Bread (*maṣṣôt*) recalls their departure in haste (vv. 33-39). The central symbol of the Festival of Booths is a reminder of how the Israelites lived in temporary dwellings when they fled from Egypt (Lev. 23:42-43). The great festivals affirm Yhwh both as the mighty saving God and creator who blesses Israel's harvest. The emphasis in Weeks is the harvest and creation, although later interpreters linked this time to the making of the covenant and the giving of the Torah at Mount Sinai, both of which happen in the third month (Exod. 19:1; Jub. 6:15-22).

Even if the Sabbath command of Leviticus 23:2 is a later addition, from a literary perspective its initial placement and separate introduction reinforce its importance. The Priestly account of creation (Gen. 1) is unique in recounting the story of creation in seven days. In six days God creates the material universe, but the seventh day is a holy day of rest (Gen. 2:1-3). The moon, the sun and the stars, the primary arbiters of time according to the ancient world, are here relativized by the seven-day creation and subordinated to it. The association with seven has a broader significance in many of Leviticus's rituals that further reinforces the sabbatical pattern. There are seven festivals in the year that climax in the seventh month. Seven also appears in the sacrificial laws, indicating the number of times blood is sprinkled. The laws of impurity frequently require Israelites to wait seven days as part of the purification from major impurity. Later in Numbers 28–29 seven plays a key role in the number of sacrifices offered during the festivals. Seven is a major integrating feature of several dimensions of the entire Priestly system (Jenson 1992:192–5). If four is the controlling number of the spatial world (the four directions, the four corners of the earth), then seven is the number that dominates holy time.

Leviticus 23 reflects in all likelihood a long history of editing. The double introduction at the beginning of the chapter (Lev. 23:2, 4) suggests that the Sabbath reference (v. 3) was a later addition. The summary of vv. 37-38 looks like a conclusion but is now followed by supplementary comments on the Festival of Booths (vv. 39-43). Numerous historical and literary questions are raised by a comparison with the other four Pentateuchal texts that give calendrical information (Exod. 23:14-17; 34:18, 21-24; Num. 28–29; Deut. 16:1-17). There is an extensive debate whether Leviticus 23 selectively edited Numbers 28–29 (Knohl 1987; Milgrom 2001:2054; Weyde 2004) or whether Numbers 28–29 was a later supplementary list supplying details about the sacrifices (Nihan 2008). Whatever the relative or absolute dating, the portrayal of the calendar presented in the two texts is largely consistent.

# The sabbatical year and the Jubilee

In Leviticus 25 the primacy of seven in marking holy time in the week (the Sabbath) and the year (the festivals of the seventh month) is extended to the seventh year and the fiftieth year ($7 \times 7 + 1$). Because the Jubilee year is to be treated as holy (v. 10), it is fitting that it begins in the autumn, after the

Day of Atonement has dealt with all accumulated impurity and sin. This is also the likely start of the sabbatical year, since it happens after the gathering in of the harvest in the autumn (v. 3). The sabbatical year thus corresponds with the agricultural year, which begins with sowing in the autumn and ends with the various harvests (Clines 1974). Many societies have 'years' that do not coincide with the calendrical year, such as the tax or academic year.

There are a few post-exilic references to the seventh year agricultural break (Neh. 10:31 [Heb. 32]; 1 Macc. 6:49, 53), but the custom could be older. In practice it depends on careful crop rotation. In the ancient world fields received very variable rainfall and were often marginally fertile, so they had to be left fallow frequently. This might well be every third year or even every other year. With the right rotation it would be possible to harvest all the fields in the sixth year (Milgrom 2001:2248–51). Bergsma (2007:103–5) suggests that such a practice encouraged a return to the Abrahamic paradigm of dependence on animals rather than grain. Furthermore, it could be a practical economic measure in providing the time and manpower to clear new fields for cultivation the following year.

But how could Israelites survive the further year of rest that came with the Jubilee? One approach is to reduce the time of observance to a more survivable period. This could happen if the forty-ninth year was the same as the fiftieth, perhaps through inclusive counting, or because fifty is simply used in a loose sense for the forty-ninth. However, this approach requires setting aside Leviticus 25:20-22, which refers to eating in the ninth year. Another solution is that of Hoenig (1969:223), who proposes a brief intercalary 'year'. Verse 8 would read 'and the days of the seven Sabbaticals of years, forty-nine'. The forty-nine days allow for a realignment of the lunar and solar calendars. However, this requires an emendation of the present text and his intercalary proposal is doubtful.

The plain reading of the text is that the fiftieth year is a full additional year, reckoned from the autumn. It coincides with the first year of the next sabbatical cycle in order to maintain the regular seven-year cycle (Leviticus 25:3 does not apply to the Jubilee, Gane 2004:433). The bumper triple harvest of the spring of the sixth year leads to two full years of not planting (autumn of year 6 to spring of year 7 = sabbatical Year; autumn of year 7 to spring of year 8 = Jubilee). This is then followed by planting in the autumn of year 8 and harvest in the spring of year 9 (= year 2 of the next sabbatical cycle). The practicality of the Jubilee is widely debated. Might it be possible with a shrewd crop rotation, or does it assume a miraculous provision by Yhwh (vv. 20-21), or was it always a theoretical provision?

The Jubilee included the remission of debts and the return of displaced families to their original homes. From a practical point of view this would provide an invaluable safety net. Farming in Israel was uncertain and risky (cf. Neh. 5:1-13). A family might find themselves in deep difficulty for a number of reasons such as natural disaster, poor management, war or corruption. Borrowing money and going into debt would quickly lead to debt enslavement and the loss of land. The Jubilee is a way to limit the consequences of unpayable debt and make a new start economically viable.

The Jubilee provisions are often compared to the similar laws of Deuteronomy 15:1-3, which however takes place in the seventh year. The usual relative dating suggests that Leviticus 25 might be correcting Deuteronomy, perhaps because a seven-yearly remission was unworkable and needed to take place less frequently. On the other hand, Bergsma (2007:136–8) argues that Deuteronomy reflects a later, urban context. Deuteronomy applies to individuals, while Leviticus 25 addresses the fate of entire households. The Jubilee legislation applies the concept of remission of debts in a creative and novel way to a rural context in which a family's land inheritance is core to Israelite identity.

There are Mesopotamian parallels to the Jubilee remission of debts. Kings sometimes proclaimed a general *mīšarum* (a 'straightening-out') when they ascended to the throne or encountered an appropriate emergency. This could include a release from debts, *andurāru*, a term cognate to Hebrew *dᵉrôr* ('release' or 'liberty'; Lev. 25:10; Isa. 61:1). As is often the case with parallels, there are as many differences as similarities. They are occasional events, rather than periodic ones, and the theological rationale of the Jubilee is missing. Even if the parallels are significant, they do not decide the debate whether the law reflects historical practice or hypothetical ideal.

Leviticus 25 reflects the successive stages of destitution for an Israelite (Chirichigno 1993:323–4): the selling of land (Lev. 25:25-34), dependency upon kin (vv. 35-38), being sold (with his family) to an Israelite (vv. 39-43), being sold (with his family) to a foreigner (vv. 47-54). The other party is leasing, not buying, the land so that it is the value of the crops until the Jubilee that is being paid. In a subsistence economy the only alternative to starvation and death is often debt slavery, which has a very different rationale and purpose than the oppressive slavery normally associated with the term. Indeed, verse 40 emphasizes that Israelites are to be treated as hired or bound labourers. The Jubilee requires a return to the ancestral land, partly because without such a source of income those who had been remitted would quickly fall back into debt. The theological rationale for the laws is stated in verse 23: 'The land shall not be sold in perpetuity, for the land is mine; with me you are but aliens and tenants.' The land is both a divine possession and a divine gift (Wright 1992:1026). The basis for this is the Exodus (vv. 42, 55). The sabbatical year and the Jubilee allow the wealthy, the slaves, the poor, the land and even the wild animals (v. 7) to acknowledge their dependence upon Yhwh and his blessing (26:3-5). Later texts link the Jubilee to other aspects of Israel's eschatological expectation, especially the coming of an anointed one (Isa. 61:1-4; 11Q13; Lk. 4:16-21).

# Leviticus 16 and the Day of Atonement

The principles underlying the sacrifices, the priesthood and the laws of impurity are given a climactic expression in Leviticus 16. The Day of Atonement (*yom hakippurim*; traditionally Yom Kippur) happens once a year on the tenth day of the seventh month (Lev. 16:29-34; 23:27). The first part of the ritual consisted of a special form of the purification offering. The second part involves the notorious scapegoat.

The unique treatment of the blood of the purification offering is appropriate for its special role. In Leviticus 4 the following rituals are specified (Figure 7). On the Day of Atonement these rites are extended to the innermost shrine, the Holy of Holies (Figure 8).

Only on this day does the High Priest enter the Holy of Holies, since a comprehensive atonement is carried out for all of the three main areas of the Tabernacle. The total number of blood manipulations is also the superlative multiple of seven, 49 (Milgrom 1991:1038–9). The closer the blood is to the presence of God, the more potent is its atoning power. The danger of such a close approach by the High Priest is highlighted by the need for incense, which protects him from full exposure to the divine presence (Lev. 16:12-13). Perhaps for the same reason he only sprinkles the blood on the cover of the ark, rather than applying it with a finger, as was the case for the other forms of the sacrifice.

The second part introduces an element found nowhere else: the scapegoat. It is integrated with the first ritual in that lots cast over the two goats decide which one is 'for the Lord' (as the purification offering for the congregation)

**Figure 7** The blood ritual of the purification offering

| Lev. 4 | Zone | Offender | Animal | Blood manipulation | Food for (Lev. 6:24-30 [Heb. 17-23]) |
|---|---|---|---|---|---|
| 3-12 | Holy Place | Anointed priest | Bull | Sprinkle in front of the curtain ×7 Put on horns of the incense altar ×4 | No one |
| 13-21 | | Congregation | Bull | | No one |
| 22-26 | Courtyard | Leader | Goat (m) | Put on horns of altar of burnt offering ×4 | Priests |
| 27-31 | | Anyone | Goat (f) | | Priests |
| 32-35 | | Anyone | Sheep (f) | | Priests |

**Figure 8** The blood ritual of the purification offering on the Day of Atonement

| Lev. 16 | Zone | Offender | Animal | Blood manipulation (total x49) | Food for |
|---|---|---|---|---|---|
| 11-16a | Holy of Holies | High priest + congregation | Bull and goat (m) | Sprinkle on front of cover ×1 Sprinkle before cover ×7 | No one |
| 16b | Holy Place | | Bull and goat (m) | [Sprinkle in front of the curtain ×7 Put on horns of the incense altar ×4] | |
| 18-19 | Courtyard | | Bull/goat (m) mixed | Put on horns of altar ×4 Sprinkle on altar ×7 | |

and which one is 'for Azazel'. The meaning and origin of Azazel are mysterious and disputed. It might mean 'departing goat' (hence scapegoat) or 'a rough place', but the correspondence with 'to Yhwh' (v. 8) suggests it was a personal being, a demon. Demons dwelt in the wilderness (Lev. 17:7) and later Jewish interpreters identified him with one of the fallen angels (1 Enoch 10:4-8; 4Q180 f1:7-8). In a move typical of biblical monotheism, the figure is emptied of all independent power and personality and becomes merely the symbolic destination for all Israel's sins and impurities. The absorption of Azazel into the Israelite world view is one reason why it is difficult to discover the background to the name and the history behind the elimination ritual.

A focus on the spatial dimension allows an integrated narrative reading of the rituals associated with the two goats (Jenson 1992:197–208; Gane 2004:278–80). The first part reflects a heightened application of the purification ritual in order to deal with the effects of Israel's impurities and transgressions on the sanctuary (Lev. 16:16). The High Priest moves into the inmost sanctuary, and then outwards again, in order to purify the outer holy place and the altar of burnt offering (vv. 16a, 18-19). The outward movement continues in the scapegoat ritual, where the goat is sent out to the chaotic wilderness, the extreme polar opposite of God's presence in the Holy of Holies. The first part emphasizes a comprehensive atonement and purification. The second makes use of very different metaphors, transfer and elimination. Unlike the one hand used for purification sacrifices, 'Aaron shall lay both his hands on the head of the live goat' (v. 21).

The problems dealt with by the two actions overlap: impurities, transgressions, sins (v. 16) and iniquities, transgressions, sins (v. 21). Some of these are dealt with regularly throughout the year, such as physical ritual impurities and sins that can be atoned for. But others can only be removed on the Day of Atonement, especially transgressions, which are defiant sins (the term is often translated 'rebellion'). It would also catch up major and possibly minor impurities that had not been purified either through oversight or through deliberate neglect. The Day of Atonement was an annual, supremely powerful double ritual that dealt with all these matters in ways that were both continuous and discontinuous with other sacrifices. It was to be a grand spring-clean, an annual rebooting of the purity system. The blood brought into the Holy of Holies purified the whole sanctuary from its accumulated impurities. It enabled a new beginning and an untainted celebration of the Festival of Booths that would shortly follow (Lev. 23:27-43).

The priests are included in the problem resolved by the Day of Atonement but raise the further question: who purifies the purifiers? The issue is perhaps acknowledged by another distinctive feature: the special clothing of the High Priest. Rather than his usual splendid garments (Lev. 8:7-9, 13) he wears four simple linen clothes that foregrounded his representative character rather than his hierarchical supremacy. The people were caught up in what he was doing: they identified with the potential deadly consequences of their sins and impurities through cessation of work and fasting (16:29).

# Reflections on holy time

The weekly, annual and more infrequent celebrations of holy days and festivals had several important functions (Klingbeil 2011). They helped provide a varied but stable set of rhythms that ordered the lives of Israelites and integrated them both with the agricultural cycle and with the distinctives of their faith in Yhwh. The festivals were means of embedding theology through heightened experiences of cult and community. The Sabbath and the great pilgrimage festivals became key markers of identity over against other cultures and theologies.

Jewish tradition has by and large retained the calendar, adding some festivals (e.g. Hannukah, Purim) and adapting those mentioned in Leviticus 23 to life outside the land. The prayers for the high holidays and the Day of Atonement build on the biblical accounts and highlight their personal and corporate significance. The coming of Christ eventually brought about revolutionary changes in the calendar. Some festivals were passed over, others added (e.g. Christmas), while some were profoundly reinterpreted in the light of Christ. Passover became Good Friday when the death of Christ achieved the purification and forgiveness of sins that lay at the heart of the Day of Atonement. The centrality of the Sabbath pattern in Judaism emphasizes how revolutionary was the move from Saturday to Sunday as the normal Christian day of worship. Pentecost was also retained as a remembrance of the gift of the Spirit (Acts 2).

The concept of holy time has been increasingly attenuated in the West in modern times. A secular world has lost the rationale for the weekly Sabbath pattern, as well as the relation of the festivals to the remembrance of God's saving acts. A weakened connection to the land has also diminished awareness of dependence on the cycle of the agricultural year. Yet there is a growing awareness of the impact of the misuse of land that has led to climate change and environmental disaster. The principle of rest and celebration that underlies the calendar of Leviticus is a significant resource in countering the ideologies of consumption and unrestrained growth. Leviticus teaches a 'wholesome materiality' (Davis 2009:82) that recognizes the interconnections between land, animals, ethics, cult and society. Flouting those limits will lead to divine judgement on every area of life (Lev. 26), as is becoming all too evident.

The Jubilee has proved inspirational for both ancients and moderns in its radical call to restoration and return. From an economic point of view the Jubilee affirms the principle that all should have secure access to the means of production (land), which also provides the incentive to work hard (Burnside 2010: 250–51). At the same time it reflects a realistic acknowledgement that this will not always work, but keeps open a way back. Along with other aspects of Leviticus, it may always have been intended to be an invitation to an imaginative and creative application to the very different situation of its readers. The Jubilee 2000 campaign sought the cancellation of the crippling sovereign debt of impoverished and exploited nations with significant success. It can also be applied to the restitution of land and resources to their original owners, the end of the exploitation of the earth, and the abolition of economic slavery (Milgrom 2001:2271).

# 8

# The Continuing Relevance of Leviticus

## Before the destruction of the Temple

The ongoing relevance for the book of Leviticus was most evident in its theological and ethical teaching, especially in Leviticus 18–20. The relevance of the rituals pertaining to the Tabernacle and the land was less obvious. For Jews it was a challenge to discern how they applied to the later Temple in Jerusalem or to a people living in exile after the Temple's destruction. For Christians the coming of Christ explained the demise of the purity laws and the sacrificial system, but the ongoing authority of the Old Testament raised the question of what to do with the texts that described these rituals in such detail.

This interpretive challenge invited the exercise of imagination and ingenuity, if not fancy. To those schooled in the historical-critical approach, many later interpretations of Leviticus can appear arbitrary and subjective. Nevertheless, they often tell us much about the broader cultural and theological world of the interpreter. The purpose of the interpretation was often to teach the faith, rather than discover the original meaning of the text. An interpretation can be both rooted in the text and move beyond it in a creative way that addressed the needs of the day. The reception history of the Bible is an area of growing interest, and the history of the interpretation of Leviticus is a fascinating window into the lives of faithful believers (Levine 1989:215–38; Grabbe 1993:101–9; Elliott 2012; Watts 2013:72–86).

It was clear to commentators that Leviticus had to be interpreted flexibly when relating it to a later age. The Tabernacle in the wilderness is not the same as the Temple in the land of Israel. The Temple Scroll from Qumran was probably edited into its present form between 150 and 160 BCE. It sets out a program for how the Temple should be constructed, festivals celebrated and purity maintained. Scholars continue to discuss how far its programme was practical, idealistic or eschatological. One important question was what level of holiness and purity was required in the Temple and in the city. Minimalist views suggested that the quality of purity needed for the Tabernacle was restricted to the precincts of the Temple, rather than all Jerusalem. But the Temple Scroll asserted the holiness of the entire city of the sanctuary and thus the necessity of maintaining a high degree of purity and undergoing purifications of a degree exceeding those required by Leviticus. For example, a man with an emission of semen requires three days' cleansing rather than just one (11Q19 45:11-12). It was also possible to interpret other scriptures in the light of Leviticus. Another Qumran text, the Genesis Apocryphon, tells how Noah offers the sacrifices set out in Leviticus (1Q20 10). His righteousness is confirmed through the fulfilment of commandments, even well before they were given at Sinai.

Philo of Alexandria (c. 20 BCE–50 CE) discussed many of the laws in Leviticus in his four books on the *Special Laws* of the Pentateuch. He sought to set out the plain meaning of the text, but he was also concerned to move beyond that to the spiritual or allegorical meaning. This was often an ethical reflection, such as how the prohibition of leaven in the peace offering (Lev. 6:17 [Heb. 6:10]) teaches that the offeror should not be puffed up and proud (*Spec. Leg.* 1.293). Some of Philo's readings are strongly influenced by his immersion in Hellenistic culture and in particular the Platonic tradition. Thus the male animal offered in the burnt offering reflects the way that the male is more complete and more dominant than the female. The rational is also of the masculine gender, whereas the irrational and the outward senses belong to the feminine (1.200-201). The primacy of the soul over the body informs his comments on the instruction to wash the feet of a sacrifice with water (Lev. 1:9). This indicates that the soul should no longer be earthbound but wing its way on high to join the ranks of God's heavenly host (*Spec. Leg.* 1.207). Another interpreter of the Pentateuchal laws was Josephus, who synthesizes and paraphrases the laws in his *Jewish Antiquities*. One creative touch, typical of Greek historiography, was putting a speech in the mouth of Moses setting out why Aaron was worthy to be ordained as priest (*Ant.* 3.188-192). He also refutes the accusation that Moses had fled from Egypt because he had been struck by leprosy. The humiliating laws of leprosy (Lev. 13–14) make this a ridiculous charge (3.265-6).

The New Testament shows that the coming of Christ led to a fundamental re-evaluation of many of the rituals of Leviticus. Gentiles did not need to keep the dietary laws of Leviticus 11 (Acts 10–11), because the new criterion of membership of the people of God was faith in Christ. The sacrificial death of Christ meant that the sacrificial system became a symbolic pointer (Rom. 3:25), rather than a necessary means of seeking God. The ethical rather than the physical aspects of purity and holiness become primary (Mk 7:1-23; Rom. 7:12). The general holiness of the people of God is highlighted, rather than the specific holiness of priests (Rom. 12:1; 1 Pet. 2:9). However, the tension between the holy status of Christians (as 'saints') and their call to live holy lives is evident in the New Testament (2 Cor. 1:1; 7:1) and reflects the same tension as is found in Leviticus.

The Epistle to the Hebrews is the only text that engages in depth with the priestly perspective of Leviticus, although it is read through the lens of the prophets and the Psalms. These have already pointed out the inadequacy of Temple worship, resulting in the need for a new covenant (Jer. 31:31-34; Heb. 8:7-13). A particularly original exposition is inspired by the mysterious appearance of Melchizedek in Psalm 110:4. This points to the need for a High Priest who is not of the Aaronic line. It is Jesus who is this High Priest after the order of Melchizekek, who offers a sacrifice for sin consisting not of the blood of goats and bulls but of his own blood (Heb. 5). The atoning work of Christ far transcends that of the Day of Atonement, for it marks not just the once-for-all sacrificial death of the Son of God, but also the bringing of the blood of the risen Lord into the heavenly sanctuary (Moffitt 2011). The author's Christian readers need to behave in a way that recognizes the obsolescence and ineffectiveness of the existing Temple and its sacrifices. Yet this is not a reason to ignore Leviticus. Only in studying in depth Israel's worship in the context of later writings can the true achievement of Christ be grasped.

# Jewish interpretation after the destruction of the Temple

The destruction of the Jerusalem Temple in 70 CE was a practical and interpretive challenge for rabbinic Judaism. The central prayer of the Jewish liturgy, the Amidah, includes a prayer for the restoration of the Temple service. Yet various practices were also regarded as the equivalent of Temple worship. One who performs acts of charity is greater than one who sacrifices all types of offerings (b. Suk 49b). Studying the laws of sacrifice is as if the sacrifices were offered (b. Men. 110a). Such study would no doubt be encouraged when taking seriously the proposal of R. Berekiah: 'If a man wishes to offer a libation upon the altar, let him fill the throat of the disciples of the wise with wine' (b. Yoma 71a). An early acquaintance with Leviticus was unavoidable when it became the set text for the initial study of Hebrew (Lev. R. 7:3). The need for adaptation to new circumstances is recognized by the comment that 'as long as the Temple stood, the altar atoned for Israel, but now a man's table atones for him' (b. Ber 55a). Temple sacrifice became the template for the frequency and weighting of public liturgical prayer. Ritual practices that didn't require the Temple became prominent, such as circumcision and the observation of the Sabbath and the festivals. With the demise of holy space, purity gained a more independent significance, rather than being a precondition for holiness.

The eleventh and twelfth centuries saw the emergence of the great Jewish commentators (Liebowitz 1980; Carasik 2009): Rashi (Rabbi Solomon ben Isaac, 1040–1105), Rashbam (Rabbi Samuel ben Meir, 1085–1158), Ibn Ezra (1089–1164) and Nahmanides (Moses ben Nahman, 1194–1270). The multiple exegetical challenges of Leviticus meant that a concern to explain the straightforward meaning of the text (the Peshat) took priority over more imaginative or applied interpretations (Midrash). For example, Rashi explains Azazel (Lev. 16:8) by its etymology, a rugged mountain with a steep cliff. Ibn Ezra was not satisfied with this and, as with other provocative comments, adopts an elusive style: 'If you have been able to understand the mystery behind the word Azazel, you will know both its secret and the secret of its name. … I shall reveal a bit of the mystery to you, allusively; when you are 33, you will know it.' This is a reference to Leviticus 17:7, 33 verses later, which mentions goat demons. Nahmanides clarifies Ibn Ezra's comment at length and assures his readers that this does not imply worship.

The dietary laws setting out what food is fit for eating (*kosher*) or not continue to this day to be one of the central markers of what it means to be a Jew. The lists of clean and unclean animals had to be extended beyond the limited biblical presentation. For example, there is no list or definition of what were clean birds. The Mishnah states that clean birds must have a crop, a gizzard which can easily be peeled off, and an extra talon (Ḥul. 3:6) Different Jewish traditions sometimes differed in their interpretation, for example regarding the cleanness of the pheasant or the turkey.

Will the system of sacrificial worship detailed in Leviticus be restored? Reformed Judaism has updated prayers to eliminate the expectation of a restored sacrificial system. Conversely, some ultra-orthodox sects in Israel have been preparing the utensils that would be needed for sacrifice in a restored Third Temple. Most Jewish interpreters find ways to acknowledge the historical and symbolic importance of sacrifice without advocating its literal re-establishment. Fine examples of this are found in the extensive excurses in Milgrom's commentary (Milgrom 1991; 2000; 2001).

# Christian interpretation

Early Christian interpreters used a variety of approaches in relating Leviticus to the life of the church. Origen (c185–253 CE) employed a threefold approach to scripture. Just as a person consists of body, soul and spirit, so scripture includes a literal, moral and spiritual meaning. Sometimes the literal is sufficient, but another meaning can be present or even required. Origen pours scorns on those who desire to interpret literally the mythical griffin (probably 'vulture' in the Hebrew) he found in his Greek translation of Leviticus 11:13 (*On First Principles* Book IV). In his homily on Leviticus 16 he describes the difference between the two sanctuaries of the Tabernacle. The visible sanctuary was open to priests, who represent the church, the priestly race. The invisible sanctuary was the object of Jesus's entry into heaven and where he takes incense and coals from the altar of burnt offering. Blessed are those, Origen proclaims, in whose heart is such a spiritual understanding and composed of such diverse sweetness of virtues that Christ fills his hands with them and offers them to the Father (Barkley 1990:196–7).

The tension between the two kinds of holiness found in Leviticus (general and particular) is found throughout the history of the church. The New Testament emphasis is almost exclusively on the general holiness of the people of God. For Paul all Christians have been sanctified by the Lord and so are saints, the holy ones (1 Cor. 1:2). They have become God's holy Temple (3:17). Yet this did not prevent churches from being constructed in ways that reflected the structured grading of the Tabernacle. A similar development is found in the language of Christian leadership. Priestly language only began to be invoked in the third century, when Cyprian applied the language of 'priest' (*sacerdos*) to bishops. The reformation marked a reaction against this perception, preferring an emphasis on the priesthood of all believers.

An influential development in medieval Christianity was the threefold analysis of biblical law into the moral, judicial and ceremonial (e.g. Thomas Aquinas *Summa* IIa, 99). The first two categories may still apply, but the third (represented by much of Leviticus) has been superseded. This distinction was taken over by Calvin (*Institutes* 4:20:14) and other reformers and encouraged a strong anti-ritualistic stance in Protestant circles. Instead, symbolic and allegorical meanings were found in the laws and rituals, often with a Christological or an ethical emphasis.

The critique of 'empty ritual' proved immensely influential in the development of Protestant critical biblical scholarship and its critique of the legalism of the Priestly writing. It also reflected the wider cultural movement towards individualistic and intellectualistic forms of faith that have been prominent in post-enlightenment Western culture. The majority of critical study over the last 200 years took over the assumptions of the secular age (Taylor 2007). The linguistic and historical analysis of the Priestly writing and the Holiness Code remained within the immanent frame, emphasizing the human dimension of the text and bracketing the transcendent claims of the text. This remains the case in many of the newer methods of study such as structuralist, rhetorical and sociological approaches.

A renewed interest in the theological interpretation of the text is a feature of some of those representing committed Jewish and Christian scholarship. The interest in theological interpretation is represented in a number of commentaries (Milgrom 2004; Radner 2008) and studies (Morales 2015; Levenson 2016). These authors seek to read Leviticus within its broader biblical context and relate it to the ongoing tradition of faith.

This has always been the case in preaching and teaching of Leviticus in churches and synagogues. Indeed, in stark contrast to the Western suspicion of Leviticus, many churches in the traditional cultures of India and Africa are fascinated by the rituals and purity laws of Leviticus. These resonate with their own practices and often result in a unique and creative interlacing of the laws of Leviticus, the New Testament transformation of those laws and the inherited culture. For example, some churches adopt aspects of the dietary laws (Jenkins 2006:50). In African Zionist churches rituals of purification restore the equilibrium of powers that sustain the order of the world, although without recourse to blood sacrifice (van Zyl 1995).

Leviticus is a great cathedral constructed by its Priestly builders over long centuries, eventually becoming a complex edifice that intrigues archaeologists, architects, believers and sceptics. The archaeologists (historical critics) seek to tell the story of how its different parts developed and merged over time into the intricate text that we know now. The architects (literary critics) explore the rich harmonies and dissonances of the final form of the building. Believing readers ponder how the building can house the living God and communicate his presence and blessing to worshippers. On the other hand secular critics worry whether the building, or at least some aspects of it, shapes for ill those who frequent it. The diversity of approaches to Leviticus is a small-scale model of the lively conversation that marks biblical studies today. Whether readers share the approach adopted in this guide or not, I hope that it indicated in some measure why so many find the book of Leviticus such a fascinating, provocative and counter-cultural gift.

# Bibliography

Anderson, G.A. (1987), *Sacrifices and Offerings in Ancient Israel: Studies in Their Social and Political Importance*, Harvard Semitic Monographs 41, Atlanta: Scholars Press.

Auld, A.G. (2003), 'Leviticus: After Exodus and before Numbers', in R. Rendtorff, R.A. Kugler, and S.S. Bartel (eds), *The Book of Leviticus: Composition and Reception*, 41–54, VTSup 93; Formation and Interpretation of Old Testament Literature 3, Leiden: Brill.

Averbeck, R.E. (2003), 'Sacrifices and Offerings', in D.W. Baker and T.D. Alexander (eds), *Dictionary of the Old Testament: Pentateuch*, 706–33, Leicester: IVP.

Balentine, S.E. (2002), *Leviticus*, Interpretation, Louisville: John Knox Press.

Barkley, G.W. (1990), *Origen: Homilies on Leviticus, 1–16*, Washington, DC: Catholic University of America Press.

Barton, J. (1984), 'Classifying Biblical Criticism', *JSOT*, 29: 19–35.

Bell, C. (1992), *Ritual Theory, Ritual Practice*, Oxford: Oxford University Press.

Bergsma, J.S. (2007), *The Jubilee from Leviticus to Qumran: A History of Interpretation*, VTSup 115, Leiden: Brill.

Berman, J. (2017), *Inconsistency in the Torah: Ancient Literary Convention and the Limits of Source Criticism*, New York: Oxford University Press.

Bigger, S.F. (1979), 'The Family Laws of Leviticus 18 in Their Setting', *JBL*, 98: 187–203.

Blenkinsopp, J. (1995), *Sage, Priest, Prophet: Religious and Intellectual Leadership in Ancient Israel*, Louisville: Westminster/John Knox.

Blenkinsopp, J. (1996), 'An Assessment of the Alleged Pre-Exilic Date of the Priestly Material in the Pentateuch', *ZAW*, 108: 495–518.

Blum, E. (1990), *Studien zur Komposition des Pentateuch*, BZAW 189, Berlin: De Gruyter.

Brownson, J.V. (2013), *Bible, Gender, Sexuality: Reframing the Church's Debate on Same-Sex Relationships*, Grand Rapids, MI: Eerdmans.

Brueggemann, W. (1997), *Theology of the Old Testament: Testimony, Dispute, Advocacy*, Minneapolis: Fortress.

Budd, P.J. (1989), 'Holiness and the Cult', in R.E. Clements (ed), *The World of Ancient Israel*, 275–98, Cambridge: Cambridge University Press.

Budd, P.J. (1996), *Leviticus*, London: Marshall Pickering.

Burkert, W. (1983), *Homo Necans: The Anthropology of Ancient Greek Sacrificial Ritual and Myth*, Berkeley: University of California Press.

Burnside, J.P. (2003), *The Signs of Sin: Seriousness of Offence in Biblical Law*, JSOTSup 364, London; New York: Sheffield Academic Press.

Burnside, J.P. (2010), *God, Justice, and Society: Aspects of Law and Legality in the Bible*, New York; Oxford: Oxford University Press.

Carasik, M. (2009), *The Commentators' Bible: The JPS Miqra'ot Gedolot: Leviticus*, Philadelphia, PA: Jewish Publication Society.

Carr, D.M. (2011), *The Formation of the Hebrew Bible: A New Reconstruction*, New York: Oxford University Press.

Chirichigno, G.C. (1993), *Debt-Slavery in Israel and Ancient Near East*, JSOTSup 141, Sheffield: Sheffield Academic Press.

Clines, D.J.A. (1974), 'The Evidence for an Autumnal New Year in Pre-Exilic Israel Reconsidered', *JBL*, 93: 22–40.

Clines, D.J.A. (1997), *The Bible and the Modern World*, Sheffield: Sheffield Academic Press.

Cody, A. (1969), *A History of Old Testament Priesthood*, Analecta Biblica 35, Rome: Pontifical Biblical Institute.

Cothey, A. (2005), 'Ethics and Holiness in the Theology of Leviticus', *JSOT*, 30: 131–51.

Cross, F.M. (1973), *Canaanite Myth and Hebrew Epic*, Cambridge, MA: Harvard University Press.

Crüsemann, F. (1996), *The Torah: Theology and Social History of Old Testament Law*, Minneapolis: Augsburg Fortress.

Davidson, R.M. (2007), *Flame of Yahweh: Sexuality in the Old Testament*, Peabody, MA: Hendrickson Publishers.

Davis, E.F. (2009), *Scripture, Culture, and Agriculture: An Agrarian Reading of the Bible*, Gammie, Cambridge: Cambridge University Press.

Dixon, T. (2003), *From Passions to Emotions: The Creation of a Secular Psychological Category*, Cambridge: Cambridge University Press.

Douglas, M. (1966), *Purity and Danger*, London: Routledge & Kegan Paul.

Douglas, M. (1995), 'Poetic Structure in Leviticus', in A. Hurvitz (ed), *Pomegranates and Golden Bells: Studies in Biblical, Jewish, and Near Eastern Ritual, Law, and Literature in Honor of Jacob Milgrom*, 239–56, Winona Lake, IN: Eisenbrauns.

Douglas, M. (1999), *Leviticus as Literature*, Oxford; New York: Oxford University Press.

Dozeman, T.B. (2017), *The Pentateuch: Introducing the Torah*, Introducing Israel's Scriptures, Minneapolis: Fortress Press.

Driver, S.R. (1913), *An Introduction to the Literature of the Old Testament*, 9th edn. Edinburgh: T&T Clark.

Duke, R.K. (2003), 'Priests, Priesthood', in *Dictionary of the Old Testament: Pentateuch*, 646–55, Leicester: IVP.

Eberhart, C.A. (2004), 'A Neglected Feature of Sacrifice in the Hebrew Bible: Remarks on the Burning Rite on the Altar', *Hebrew Annual Review*, 97: 485–93.

Ellens, D.L. (2008), *Women in the Sex Texts of Leviticus and Deuteronomy: A Comparative Conceptual Analysis*, LHBOTS 458, New York: T&T Clark.

Elliger, K. (1966), *Leviticus*, Handbuch zum Alten Testament 4, Tübingen: Mohr Siebeck.

Elliott, M.W. (2012), *Engaging Leviticus: Reading Leviticus Theologically with Its Past Interpreters*, Eugene, OR: Cascade Books.

Feder, Y. (2010), 'On Kuppuru, Kippēr and Etymological Sins That Cannot Be Wiped Away', *VT*, 60: 535–45.

Feinstein, E.L. (2014), *Sexual Pollution in the Hebrew Bible*, Oxford: Oxford University Press.

Fleming, D.E. (1998), 'The Biblical Tradition of Anointing Priests', *JBL*, 117: 410–14.

Fretheim, T.E. (1968), 'The Priestly Document: Anti-Temple?' *VT*, 18: 313–29.

Gane, R.E. (2004), *Leviticus, Numbers*, The NIV Application Commentary, Grand Rapids, MI: Zondervan.

Gane, R.E. (2005), *Cult and Character: Purification Offerings, Day of Atonement, and Theodicy*, Winona Lake, IN: Eisenbrauns.

Geller, S. (1992), 'Blood Cult: Toward a Literary Theology of the Priestly Work of the Pentateuch', *Prooftexts*, 12: 97–124.

Gemser, B. (1953), 'The Importance of the Motive Clause in Old Testament Law', in *Congress Volume, Copenhagen, 1953*, 50–66, VTSup 1, Leiden: Brill.

Gerstenberger, E. (1996), *Leviticus: A Commentary*, OTL, Louisville, KY: Westminster John Knox Press.

Gese, H. (1981), 'Atonement', in *Essays on Biblical Theology*, 93–116, Minneapolis: Augsburg.

Gilders, W.K. (2004), *Blood Ritual in the Hebrew Bible: Meaning and Power*, Baltimore: The Johns Hopkins University Press.

Ginsbursky, L. (2009), 'The Idea of Sin-Impurity: The Dead Sea Scrolls in the Light of Leviticus', PhD diss., University of Cambridge, Cambridge.

Girard, R. (1972), *Violence and the Sacred*, Baltimore: Johns Hopkins University Press.

Gorman, F.H. (1990), *The Ideology of Ritual: Space, Time and Status in the Priestly Theology*, JSOTSup 91, Sheffield: Sheffield Academic Press.

Gorman, F.H. (1997), *Divine Presence and Community: A Commentary on the Book of Leviticus*, International Theological Commentary, Grand Rapids: Eerdmans.

Grabbe, L.L. (1993), *Leviticus*, OTG, Sheffield: Sheffield Academic Press.

Grabbe, L.L. (2003), 'The Priests in Leviticus – Is the Medium the Message?' in R. Rendtorff, R.A. Kugler and S.S. Bartel (eds), *The Book of Leviticus: Composition and Reception*, 207–24, VTSup 93; Formation and Interpretation of Old Testament Literature 3, Leiden: Brill.

Greenstein, E.L. (1989), 'Deconstruction and Biblical Narrative', *Prooftexts*, 9: 43–71.

Gruber, M.I. (1987), 'Women in the Cult According to the Priestly Code', in E.S. Fredrichs (ed), *Judaic Perspectives on Ancient Israel*, 35–48, Philadelphia: Fortress.

Haran, M. (1978), *Temples and Temple-Service in Ancient Israel*, Oxford: Clarendon Press.

Haran, M. (1981), 'Behind the Scenes of History – Determining the Date of the Priestly Source', *JBL*, 100: 321–33.

Haran, M. (2008), 'Ezekiel, P, and the Priestly School', *VT*, 58 (2): 211–18.

Hartley, J.E. (1992), *Leviticus*, Word, Waco, TX: Word.

Hasel, G.F. (1988), '"New Moon and Sabbath" in Eight Century Israelite Prophetic Writings (Isa 1:13; Hos 2:13; Amos 8:5)', in M. Augustin and K.-D. Schunck (eds), *Wünschet Jerusalem Frieden: Iosot Congress Jerusalem 1986*, 37–64, Beiträge zur Erforschung des Alten Testaments und des Antiken Judentums 13, Frankfurt: Peter Lang.

Heschel, A.J. (1951), *The Sabbath: Its Meaning for Modern Man*, New York: Farrar, Straus & Giroux.

Hieke, T. (2014), *Levitikus 1–15*, HThKAT, Freiburg: Herder.

Hieke, T. (2014), *Levitikus 16–27*, HThKAT, Freiburg: Herder.

Hoenig, S.B. (1969), 'Sabbatical Years and the Year of Jubilee', *Jewish Quarterly Review*, 59: 222–36.

Houston, W.J. (1993), *Purity and Monotheism: Clean and Unclean Animals in Biblical Law*, JSOTSup 140, Sheffield: JSOT Press.

Hundley, M.B. (2011), *Keeping Heaven on Earth: Safeguarding the Divine Presence in the Priestly Tabernacle*, FAT 2/50, Tübingen: Mohr Siebeck.

Hundley, M.B. (2013), 'Sacred Spaces, Objects, Offerings, and People in the Priestly Texts: A Reappraisal', *JBL*, 132: 749–67.

Hurvitz, A. (1982), *A Linguistic Study of the Relationship between the Priestly Source and the Book of Ezekiel: A New Approach to an Old Problem*, Cahiers de la Revue Biblique 20, Paris: J. Gabalda.

Hurvitz, A. (1988), 'Dating the Priestly Source in Light of the Historical Study of Biblical Hebrew. A Century after Wellhausen', *ZAW*, 100 Supplement: 88–100.

Hurvitz, A. (2000), 'Once Again: The Linguistic Profile of the Priestly Material in the Pentateuch and Its Historical Age – a Response to J. Blenkinsopp', *ZAW*, 112: 180–91.

Janowski, B. (1982), *Sühne als Heilsgeschehen: Studien zur Sühnetheologie der Priesterschrift und zur Wurzel Kpr im Alten Orient und im Alten Testament*, Wissenschaftliche Monographien zum Alten und Neuen Testament 55, Neukirchen: Neukirchener Verlag.

Janzen, D. (2004), *The Social Meanings of Sacrifice in the Hebrew Bible: A Study of Four Writings*, BZAW 344, Berlin: Walter de Gruyter.

Janzen, W. (1994), *Old Testament Ethics: A Paradigmatic Approach*, Louisville, KY: Westminster John Knox.

Jenkins, P. (2006), *The New Faces of Christianity: Believing the Bible in the Global South*, New York: Oxford University Press.

Jenson, P.P. (1992), *Graded Holiness: A Key to the Priestly Conception of the World*, JSOTSup 106, Sheffield: JSOT Press.

Jenson, P.P. (2003), 'Holiness in the Priestly Writings of the Old Testament', in S.C. Barton (ed), *Holiness: Past and Present*, 93–121, Edinburgh: T&T Clark.

Jenson, P.P. (2010), 'Snakes and Ladders: Weighing and Ordering Biblical Law', in K. Dell (ed), *Ethical and Unethical in the Old Testament: God and Humans in Dialogue*, 187–207, LHBOTS 528, New York: T&T Clark.

Joosten, J. (1996), *People and Land in the Holiness Code: An Exegetical Study of the Ideational Framework of the Law in Leviticus 17–26*, VTSup 67, Leiden; New York: Brill.

Joosten, J. (2016), 'Diachronic Linguistics and the Date of the Pentateuch', in J.C. Gertz (ed), *The Formation of the Pentateuch: Bridging the Academic Cultures of Europe, Israel, and North America*, 327–44, Tübingen: Mohr Siebeck.

Kazen, T. (2015), 'Purity and Persia', in R.E. Gane and A. Taggar-Cohen (eds), *Current Issues in Priestly and Related Literature: The Legacy of Jacob Milgrom and Beyond*, 435–62, Resources for Biblical Study 82, Atlanta: SBL Press.

Kim, Y.S. (2006), 'Lex Talionis in Exod 21: 22–25 – Its Origin and Context', *The Journal of Hebrew Scriptures*, 6: 1–11.

Kiuchi, N. (1987), *The Purification Offering in the Priestly Literature: Its Meaning and Function*, JSOTSup 36, Sheffield: JSOT Press.

Kiuchi, N. (2007), *Leviticus*, Apollos, Nottingham: InterVarsity Press.

Klawans, J. (2000), *Impurity and Sin in Ancient Judaism*, Oxford; New York: Oxford University Press.

Klawans, J. (2006), *Purity, Sacrifice, and the Temple: Symbolism and Supersessionism in the Study of Ancient Judaism*, Oxford: Oxford University Press.

Klingbeil, G.A. (2011), '"Of Clocks and Calendars": The Cohesive Function of Time in Biblical Ritual Source', *Biblische Zeitschrift*, 55: 21–34.

Knohl, I. (1987), 'The Priestly Torah Versus the Holiness School: Sabbath and the Festivals', *Hebrew College Union Annual*, 58: 65–117.

Knohl, I. (1995), *The Sanctuary of Silence: The Priestly Torah and the Holiness School*, Minneapolis: Fortress.

Koehler, L. (1957), *Theology of the Old Testament*, trans. A.S. Todd, London: Lutterworth.

Kugler, R.A. (1997), 'Holiness, Purity, the Body and Society: The Evidence for Theological Conflict in Leviticus', *JSOT*, 76: 3–27.

Kugler, R.A. (2009), 'Priests and Levites', *New Interpreter's Dictionary of the Bible*, 4: 596–613.

Lakoff, G. and Johnson, M. (1999), *Philosophy in the Flesh: The Embodied Mind and Its Challenge to Western Thought*, New York: Basic Books.

Lakoff, G. and Johnson, M. (2003), *Metaphors We Live By*, Chicago, IL: University of Chicago Press.

Leithart, P.J. (1999), 'Attendants of Yahweh's House: Priesthood in the Old Testament', *JSOT*, 85: 3–24.

Lemos, T.M. (2013), 'Where There Is Dirt, Is There System? Revisiting Biblical Purity Constructions', *JSOT*, 37: 265–94.

Levenson, J.D. (2016), *The Love of God: Divine Gift, Human Gratitude, and Mutual Faithfulness in Judaism*, Library of Jewish Ideas, Princeton: Princeton University Press.

Levine, B.A. (1965), 'The Descriptive Tabernacle Texts of the Pentateuch', *JAOS*, 85: 307–18.

Levine, B.A. (1989), *Leviticus*, JPS Torah Commentary, Philadelphia: Jewish Publication Society.

Liebowitz, N. (1980), *Studies in Vayiqra (Leviticus)*, trans. A. Newman, Jerusalem: World Zionist Organization.

Lipka, H. (2010), 'Profaning the Body: Ḥll [Hebrew Characters] and the Concept of Loss of Personal Holiness in H', in S.T. Kamionkowski and W. Kim (eds), *Bodies, Embodiment, and Theology of the Hebrew Bible*, 90–113, LHBOTS 465, New York: T&T Clark.

Liss, H. (2006), 'The Imaginary Sanctuary: The Priestly Code as an Example of Fictional Literature in the Hebrew Bible', in O. Lipschitz and M. Oeming (eds), *Judah and the Judeans in the Persian Period*, 663–89, Winona Lake, IN: Eisenbrauns.

Luciani, D. (2005), *Le Lévitique, éthique et esthétique*, connaître la Bible, Bruxelles: Lumen Vitae.

Lyons, M.A. (2009), *From Law to Prophecy: Ezekiel's Use of the Holiness Code*, LHBOTS 507, London: T&T Clark.

MacDonald, N. (2012), 'The Hermeneutics and Genesis of the Red Cow Ritual', *Harvard Theological Review*, 105: 351–71.

Magonet, J. (1996), '"But If It Is a Girl She Is Unclean for Twice Seven Days..." the Riddle of Leviticus 12.5', in J.F.A. Sawyer (ed), *Reading Leviticus: A Conversation with Mary Douglas*, 144–52, Sheffield: Sheffield Academic Press.

Marx, A. (1989), 'Sacrifice pour les péchés ou rite de passage? Quelques
    rêflexions sur la fonction du *ḥaṭṭāʾt*, *RB*, 96: 27–48.
Marx, A. (2001), 'L'impureté selon P. Une lecture théologique', *Biblica*, 82:
    363–84.
Marx, A. (2005), *Les systèmes sacrificiels de l'ancien testament: Formes et
    fonctions du culte sacrificiel à Yhwh*, VTSup 105, Leiden: Brill.
Mason, S.D. (2008), *'Eternal Covenant' in the Pentateuch: The Contours of
    an Elusive Phrase*, T&T Clark Library of Biblical Studies, New York: T&T
    Clark.
Meshel, N.S. (2014), *The Grammar of Sacrifice: A Generativist Study of the
    Israelite Sacrificial System in the Priestly Writings with the Grammar of S*,
    New York: Oxford University Press.
Meyers, C.L. (1988), *Discovering Eve: Ancient Israelite Women in Context*, New
    York: Oxford University Press.
Milgrom, J. (1976), 'Israel's Sanctuary: The Priestly "Picture of Dorian Gray"',
    *RB*, 83: 390–9.
Milgrom, J. (1991, 2000, 2001), *Leviticus, 3 Vols.*, Anchor Bible, New York:
    Doubleday.
Milgrom, J. (1996), 'The Changing Concept of Holiness in the Pentateuchal
    Codes with Emphasis on Leviticus 19', in J.F.A. Sawyer (ed), *Reading
    Leviticus: A Conversation with Mary Douglas*, 65–75, JSOTSup 227,
    Sheffield: Sheffield Academic Press.
Milgrom, J. (2004), *Leviticus: A Book of Ritual and Ethics*, Continental
    Commentaries, Minneapolis: Fortress Press.
Mizrahi, N. (2011), 'The History and Linguistic Background of Two Hebrew
    Titles for the High Priest', *JBL*, 130: 687–705.
Moffitt, D.M. (2011), *Atonement and the Logic of Resurrection in the Epistle to
    the Hebrews*, NovTSup 141, Leiden: Brill.
Morales, L.M. (2015), *Who Shall Ascend the Mountain of the Lord? A Biblical
    Theology of the Book of Leviticus*, New Studies in Biblical Theology, Downers
    Grove, IL: Apollos, InterVarsity Press.
Nelson, R.D. (1993), *Raising up a Faithful Priest: Community and Priesthood in
    Biblical Theology*, Louisville, KY: Westminster John Knox.
Nihan, C. (2007), *From Priestly Torah to Pentateuch: A Study in the
    Composition of the Book of Leviticus*, FAT II/25, Tübingen: Mohr Siebeck.
Nihan, C. (2008), 'Israel's Festival Calendars in Leviticus 23, Numbers 28–29
    and the Formation of "Priestly" Literature', in T. Römer (ed), *The Books of
    Leviticus and Numbers*, 177–231, Bibliotheca Ephemeridum Theologicarum
    Lovaniensium 215, Leuven: Peeters.
Nihan, C. (2013), 'Forms and Functions of Purity in Leviticus', in C. Frevel
    and C. Nihan (eds), *Purity and the Forming of Religious Traditions in the*

*Ancient Mediterranean World and Ancient Judaism*, 311–67, Dynamics in the History of Religions 3, Leiden: Brill.

Nihan, C. (2015), 'The Templization of Israel in Leviticus: Some Remarks on Blood Disposal and Kipper', in F. Landy, L. Trevaskis and B. Bibb (eds), *Text, Time and Temple: Literary, Historical and Ritual Studies in Leviticus*, 94–130, Hebrew Bible Monographs 64, Sheffield: Sheffield Phoenix Press.

Noth, M. (1965), *Leviticus*, trans. J.E. Anderson, OTL, London: SCM.

Olyan, S.M. (1994), '"And with a Male You Shall Not Lie the Lying Down of a Woman": On the Meaning and Significance of Leviticus 18:22 and 20:13', *Journal of the History of Sexuality*, 5: 179–206.

Olyan, S.M. (2000), *Rites and Rank: Hierarchy in Biblical Representations of Cult*, Princeton, NJ: Princeton University Press.

Olyan, S.M. (2008), 'Mary Douglas's Holiness/Wholeness Paradigm: Its Potential for Insight and Its Limitations', *The Journal of Hebrew Scriptures*, 8.

Oppenheim, A.L. (1977), *Ancient Mesopotamia: Portrait of a Dead Civilization*, rev edn. Chicago: University of Chicago Press.

Otto, R. (1959), *The Idea of the Holy*, trans. J.W. Harvey, Harmondsworth: Penguin.

Radner, E. (2008), *Leviticus*, Brazos Theological Commentary, Grand Rapids, MI: Brazos Press.

Rainey, A.F. (1970), 'The Order of Sacrifices in Old Testament Ritual Texts', *Bib*, 51: 485–98.

Regev, E. (2001), 'Priestly Dynamic Holiness and Deuteronomic Static Holiness', *VT*, 51: 243–61.

Rehm, M.D. (1992), 'Levites and Priests', *ABD*, IV: 297–310.

Rendtorff, R. (2003), 'Leviticus 16 Als Mitte Der Tora', *Biblical Interpretation*, 11: 252–8.

Rendtorff, R. (2004), *Leviticus 1,1 – 10,20*, Biblischer Kommentar: Altes Testament 3.1, Neukirchner-Vluyn: Neukirchener Verlag.

Rhyder, J. (2019), *Centralizing the Cult: The Holiness Legislation in Leviticus 17–26*, FAT 134, Tübingen: Mohr Siebeck.

Ricœur, P. (1967), *The Symbolism of Evil*, trans. E. Buchanan, Boston: Beacon.

Rooke, D.W. (2000), *Zadok's Heirs: The Role and Development of the High Priesthood in Ancient Israel*, Oxford Theological Monographs, Oxford: Oxford University Press.

Ruane, N.J. (2013), *Sacrifice and Gender in Biblical Law*, New York: Cambridge University Press.

Ruwe, A. (1999), *'Heiligkeitsgesetz' und 'Priesterschrift': Literaturgeschichtliche und Rechtssystematische Untersuchungen zu Leviticus 17,1-26,2*, FAT 26, Tübingen: Mohr Siebeck.

Schwartz, B.J. (2000), 'Israel's Holiness: The Torah Traditions', in M. Poorthuis
    and J. Schwartz (eds), *Purity and Holiness: The Heritage of Leviticus*, 47–59,
    Jewish and Christian Perspectives Series 2, Leiden: Brill.

Sklar, J. (2005), *Sin, Impurity, Sacrifice, Atonement: The Priestly Conceptions*,
    Hebrew Bible Monographs 2, Sheffield: Sheffield Phoenix Press.

Sonderegger, K. (2015), *Systematic Theology. Volume 1, the Doctrine of God*,
    Minneapolis: Fortress Press.

Tate, W.R. (2008), *Biblical Interpretation: An Integrated Approach*, 3rd edn.
    Peabody, MA: Hendrickson Publishers.

Taylor, C. (1989), *Sources of the Self: The Making of the Modern Identity*,
    Cambridge: Cambridge University Press.

Taylor, C. (2007), *A Secular Age*, Cambridge, MA: Belknap Press of Harvard
    University Press.

Trevaskis, L.M. (2011), *Holiness, Ethics and Ritual in Leviticus*, Sheffield:
    Sheffield Phoenix Press.

Tucker, P.N. (2017), *The Holiness Composition in the Book of Exodus*, FAT 98 2
    Reihe, Tübingen: Mohr Siebeck.

van Zyl, D.C. (1995), 'In Africa Theology Is Not Thought Out but Danced Out
    – on the Theological Significance of Old Testament Symbolism and Rituals
    in African Zionist Churches', *OTE*, 8: 425–38.

Wagner, A. (2018), *God's Body: The Anthropomorphic God in the Old
    Testament*, New York: Bloomsbury Academic.

Wagner, V. (1974), 'Zur Existenz des Sogenannten "Heiligkeitsgesetztes"', *ZAW*,
    86: 307–16.

Walsh, J.T. (2001), 'Leviticus 18:22 and 20:13: Who Is Doing What to Whom?'
    *JBL*, 120: 201–9.

Warning, W. (1999), *Literary Artistry in Leviticus*, Biblical Interpretation Series
    35, Leiden: Brill.

Watts, J.W. (2007), *Ritual and Rhetoric in Leviticus: From Sacrifice to Scripture*,
    Cambridge: Cambridge University Press.

Watts, J.W. (2013), *Leviticus 1-10*, Historical Commentary on the Old
    Testament, Leuven: Peeters.

Webb, W.J. (2001), *Slaves, Women & Homosexuals: Exploring the Hermeneutics
    of Cultural Analysis*, Downers Grove, IL: InterVarsity Press.

Wehr, K. (2011), 'Understanding Ritual Purity and Sin in the Churching of
    Women: From Ontological to Pedagogical to Eschatological', *St Vladimir's
    Theological Quarterly*, 55: 85–105.

Weinfeld, M. (1972), *Deuteronomy and the Deuteronomic School*, Oxford:
    Oxford University Press.

Wellhausen, J. (1885), *Prolegomena to the History of Israel*, trans. J.S. Black and
    A. Menzies, Edinburgh: Adam & Charles Black.

Wenham, G.J. (1979), *The Book of Leviticus*, New International Commentary on the Old Testament, Grand Rapids: Eerdmans.

Wenham, G.J. (1983), 'Why Does Sexual Intercourse Defile (Lev 15 18)?' *ZAW*, 95: 432–4.

Weyde, K.W. (2004), *The Appointed Festivals of Yhwh: The Festival Calendar in Leviticus 23 and the Sukkot Festival in Other Biblical Texts*, FAT 2/4, Tübingen: Mohr Siebeck.

Whitekettle, R. (1991), 'Leviticus 15.18 Reconsidered: Chiasm, Spatial Structure and the Body', *JSOT*, 49: 31–45.

Whitekettle, R. (1995), 'Leviticus 12 and the Israelite Woman: Ritual Process, Liminality, and the Womb', *ZAW*, 107: 393–408.

Willis, T.M. (2009), *Leviticus*, Nashville: Abingdon Press.

Wright, C.J.H. (1992), 'Jubilee, Year Of', *ABD*, III: 102–30.

Wright, D.P. (1987), *The Disposal of Impurity*, SBLDS 101, Atlanta: Scholars Press.

Wright, D.P. (1991), 'The Spectrum of Priestly Impurity', in G.A. Anderson and S.M. Olyan (eds), *Priesthood and Cult in Ancient Israel*, 150–81, JSOTSup 125, Sheffield: Sheffield Academic Press.

Wright, D.P. (1999), 'Holiness in Leviticus and Beyond: Differing Perspectives', *Interpretation*, 53: 351–64.

Wright, D.P. (2012), 'Ritual Theory, Ritual Texts, and the Priestly-Holiness Writings of the Pentateuch', in S.M. Olyan (ed), *Social Theory and the Study of Israelite Religion: Essays in Retrospect and Prospect*, 195–216, Leiden: Brill.

Zenger, E. and Frevel, C. (1999), 'Das Buch Levitikus als Teltext der Tora/des Pentateuch: Eine Synchrone Lektüre Mit Kanonischer Perspektive', in H.-J. Fabry and H.-W. Jüngling (eds), *Levitikus als Buch*, 47–83, Bonner biblische Beiträge 119, Berlin: Philo.

Zimmerli, W. (1965), *The Law and the Prophets: A Study of the Meaning of the Old Testament*, Oxford: Blackwell.

# Author Index

# Subject Index